The Best of
Steptoe and Son

The Best of
Steptoe and Son

Written by
Ray Galton and Alan Simpson

Pan Books
London, Sydney and Auckland

First published in Great Britain in 1988 by
Robson Books Ltd, London
This edition published 1989 by Pan Books Ltd,
Cavaye Place, London SW10 9PG
9 8 7 6 5 4 3 2
© Ray Galton and Alan Simpson 1988
Drawings by K. J. Collins
ISBN 0 330 30997 8

Photoset by Parker Typesetting Service, Leicester
Printed and bound in Great Britain by
Cox & Wyman Ltd, Reading

Contents

Introduction

It was in 1962 that a reluctant Hercules was first backed into the shafts of his cart and driven across the cobblestones of the scrapyard, through the gates and into Oil Drum Lane, Shepherd's Bush, and in the process pulling Harry H. Corbett and Wilfrid Brambell into instant stardom. Over the years of totting on their weekly round they reached a clientèle of up to twenty-eight million customers.

It all began a year after our split with Tony Hancock, whose television and radio shows we had been writing for nearly ten years. Tom Sloan, then the Head of Light Entertainment at the BBC and faced with the prospect of no more Hancock, suddenly invited us to lunch. The importance of this meeting was magnified dramatically when the venue suggested was a well-known one-star Michelin restaurant in the West End of London instead of the usual BBC canteen. And when, further, he chose the 1955 La Tâche, Domaine de la Romanée-Conti, rather than the house red, we thought to ourselves 'Allo, Allo'! (Not the 'Allo, Allo' made famous by David Croft and Jeremy Lloyd two decades later but the cockney 'Allo, Allo' meaning 'Aye, aye, what's he after then?') It was soon made clear. Not even waiting for the *Loup de mer grillé farci au fenouil flambé au Pernod* he steamed straight in.

'What do you want to do now?' he said.

'Get stuck into the La Tâche,' we said, fearful that he would send it back on the grounds that red wine does not go with the fish. Our fears were groundless.

'No, man,' he said. 'I mean professionally-wise. What are you two scribes going to pen for us next?' making in his quaint English way an honourable stab at the latest American show-business vernacular. Ignoring our suggestions as always, he proceeded to offer us something that hitherto writers had only dreamt about. Money. Plus the offer of our own series. The title 'Comedy Playhouse'. The terms of reference – ten half-hours of prime-time television to do with that which we would like to do as we wish with in the first place. (That's what comes of trying not to end a sentence with a preposition!) Anything we wanted. Be in them, direct them, sketch show, situation comedy, whatever we decided. Such a proposition had never before been put to mere writers. Up until then comedy writers were those morose individuals who sometimes turned up for rehearsals thus preventing the actors from changing the lines until after they'd gone. It was an offer we could not refuse.

'OK, man,' we said, 'let's run it up a flagpole and see who salutes it.' (Just to show that we were just as *au courant* transatlantic-wise as what he was.) We decided that we would like to do a series of separate half-hour playlets with a different cast each week. That way we could work with actors rather than comedians. As any comedy writer will tell you, actors are much better house-trained. They don't go through the script counting the laughs, they just learn the lines and get on with it. Tom Sloan thought that was a fine idea. The bargain was struck, the deal agreed, and the hands shaken. Whereupon he called the *sommelier* over, asked to see the wine waiter, sent back the unopened bottle of La Tâche and ordered a bottle of the house red. A lesson well learnt. We subsequently never agreed a deal with the BBC until we were absolutely certain that we couldn't force down one more slug of Bas Armagnac, not stick another Monte Cristo behind the earhole.

And so the writer's dream began. Ten weeks of our own show. Everything went smoothly until episode four when we dried up.

'What about a series of three?' we said.

'What about being sued for breach of contract?' he said.

Appreciating the strength of his argument we went back to the typewriter.

We will now let you into a little trade secret. Our technique when stuck was to amuse ourselves with facetious suggestions for an opening scene.

'Two rat catchers laying traps in the Queen's bedroom.'

'Two nuns doing synchronized swimming.'

It was always two something or other.

'Two rag and bone men . . .' started Ray.

'No, come on, let's be serious,' said Alan, 'stop messing about,' clinging to a bygone successful catchphrase like a child clinging to its comfort blanket. Then, three hours later:

'I'm serious,' said Ray.

'Oh, all right then,' said Alan, and started typing. 'Act 1, scene 1, Wembley pool. Two nuns are discovered taking off their habits and . . .'

'No, no, no, not them. The two rag and bone men.'

And thus history was made. We started writing. First rag and bone man. Second rag and bone man. In the yard. Arguing about the day's totting. No situation. No plot. We didn't know who they were, what age they were. Were they friends? Relatives? If so, what? Brothers, cousins? After ten pages of a twenty-page script we stopped. Where were we going? We had to decide. Who were they? What is their relationship? Something in the dialogue we'd already written indicated that one was older than the other, but the obvious relationship eluded us for ages. Then it came. We'd reached the part in the script where one rag and bone man was pouring dregs from wine bottles collected from the round into various other bottles lined up on the sideboard thus making up his wine cellar. It was a label in the mind's eye that did it. Bouchard Père et Fils. That's it. That's who they are. Father and son. He's got it. By Jove, he's got it. But wait . . . the son. He's not young. He's quite old. Thirty-eight, nine. He can't get away. He's trapped. The old man won't let him go. Emotional blackmail. That was the breakthrough. The alchemy. The simple formula that turns base metal into gold. The rest of the script was easy. It was called 'The Offer'. It finished with the son trying to leave home to take up the mysterious 'offer' he's received. He's piled all his belongings on the cart. But his father owns the horse and won't let him have it. The son tries to pull the cart himself, but isn't strong enough. He must get away, but he can't. He breaks down in tears and is finally led gently back into the house by his father. 'I'm still going. I'm not stopping.' 'Of course you're not, you can go tomorrow.' But we know he won't. He never will. And that was it as far as we were concerned. A one-off. On to the next 'Comedy Playhouse'.

Before moving on though we had to cast the rag and bone men.

A phone call to Duncan Wood the producer.

'What's the availability on Harry H. Corbett and Wilfrid Brambell?'

'I'll ring you back.'

The more we thought about it, the more it was the perfect casting. Harry H. Corbett was then the actor that everybody in the business most admired. Not so well known to the general public but in the profession considered to be one of the most exciting actors on the English stage. And an innovator. He and Joan Littlewood had started the Theatre Workshop in Stratford and he had founded the Langham Group, an experimental company playing Ibsen, Shaw, Strindberg, etc, on BBC television in the 50s. Harry was as influential in his sphere as Orson Welles had been with the Mercury Theatre company in America. Other actors would rush to a TV set whenever Harry was on and would gather and analyse the performance afterwards. He was then a leading exponent of the Method School of acting, the English Marlon Brando. Now he is only remembered as Harold Steptoe, but it should never be forgotten what a remarkable influence he was on the acting profession all those years ago.

The point was, would he play the son? Would he *want* to do it even if he was available? The world was his oyster. Everybody wanted to work with him. Then came the word. He's doing a season at the Bristol Old Vic. *Henry IV*, Parts I and II. Send him the script anyway, you never know. That was the best thing we ever did. The word came back. Henry IV has abdicated for one week in order to do it. From a King of England to a rag and bone man in seven days. The biggest come-down since the last Emperor of China.

Wilfrid Brambell was a natural choice for the older man. Although only fifty at the time he specialized in old men. We had seen Wilfrid in two plays on TV playing down-and-out pensioners: 'Too Many Mansions' and 'No Fixed Abode'. He was perfect. In real life a dapper man, exquisitely dressed and beautifully spoken. The complete antithesis of his screen persona as Albert Steptoe. In fact after the shows were recorded, he would emerge from the studio totally unrecognizable in his hand-made suit and teeth. Ever the complete professional he had his street teeth and his Steptoe teeth, the latter an old rendered-down pair of blackened stumps that were kept in a glass of gin and tonic (his favourite) in the prop room until required the following week. He too was a product of the legitimate theatre, having started at the Abbey Theatre in Dublin. It is interesting that two of the most successful Cockney characters on television were played by a Dubliner and a Mancunian.

'The Offer' was a great success and the aforementioned Tom Sloan immediately wanted a series. We said no. This time the La Tâche did get opened. But still we refused on the grounds that we didn't want to get involved in a long-running show with the same cast each week so soon after having finished ten years with Tony Hancock. Besides, we said it was only a one-off and it would never make a series. We were right there. It ran to eight series. The last show was made in 1974 but it is still playing all over the world in both the original version and several foreign language reproductions. Notably Sanford and Son (USA), Stiefbeen en Zoon (Holland) and Albert og Herbert (Sweden).

We don't know where *they* got their names from but ours came from a little shop sign that caught our eye in Richmond, Surrey. A little old musty photographic shop in a narrow side street. Steptoe and Figge. Not for one moment did we consider calling it Figge and Son.

RAY GALTON AND ALAN SIMPSON

Cuckoo In The Nest

First transmission 21 December 1970

Cuckoo In The Nest featured
Kenneth J. Warren as Arthur
and was produced by Duncan Wood

SCENE 1
The Steptoes' lounge. Harold and Albert are playing chess. The board is laid out with some chess pieces and some other objects standing in for chess pieces. Harold makes a move, moving a thimble. Albert makes a move, moving a miniature liqueur bottle.

SCENE 2
The street outside the Steptoes' yard. A man gets out of a taxi, takes two suitcases and enters the yard.

SCENE 3
The lounge. Albert picks up a nut from by his side, cracks it and eats it.

Harold: Oi, that's my pawn you've just eaten.
Albert: Was it? I'd taken it anyway. (*He moves the salt cellar*)
Harold: Now what do you think you're doing?
Albert: I'm moving my queen.
Harold: That's not your queen. That's my bishop.
Albert: The salt cellar is my queen.
Harold: No, it's not. The pepper pot is your queen. How can we play a proper game if you don't know what your pieces are? Have you been moving anything else of mine?
Albert: Well, I don't know now. Is that egg cup yours?
Harold: Yes.
Albert: Oh. Well, I've moved that. Twice.

1

Harold: That's my king's rook. Oh well, that's it, isn't it? You've cocked up my Sicilian defence. I mean, there's no point in carrying on. I was trying out Novachensky's opening gambit from the World Championships. No wonder it wasn't coming off. Oh, it's no good, we'll have to get a proper set if we're going to play.
(There is a knock at the door)
Harold: Go on. Set them up. We'll give it another try. *(He goes out of the room)*

SCENE 4
The hall. Harold opens the front door. Arthur is standing there.

Arthur: Good day to you. Does Mr Albert Steptoe live here?
Harold: Yes. Yes, he does.
Arthur: So the old feller's still alive, then?
Harold: Yes, yes, he's still alive. Just.
Arthur: Good. Well, don't let's stand here like a couple of raw prawns. *(He comes in)*
Harold: Oh. You'd better come in. He's in the lounge. This way. *(He leads the way into the lounge)*

SCENE 5
The lounge.

Arthur: *(looks round)* Strewth.
Harold: *(to Albert)* There's a gentleman to see you.
(Albert gets up. He looks at Arthur, obviously doesn't recognize him)
Arthur: Well, well, well.
Albert: Who are you?
Arthur: You don't recognize me, do you?
Albert: No.
Arthur: Well, it's not surprising. You haven't seen me for forty-five years. I wasn't knee high to an abo's Y-fronts when I left. I'm Arthur.
(Albert sits down, looking at him)
Albert: Arthur? Arthur?
Arthur: Yeah, Arthur.
Albert: *(recognition slowly dawns)* Arthur. Arthur!
Arthur: Yeah.

2

Albert: Arthur! It can't be. Not Arthur?

Arthur: Arthur – yeah, Arthur.

Albert: Arthur. Harold, it's Arthur.

Harold: Is it?

Albert: I don't believe it – after all these years. Little Arthur.

Arthur: There, there, old timer, don't get upset. Let's have a Captain Cook at you. *(Holds Albert at arm's length)* Yeah, you're just the way I thought you'd be. A bit older, a bit smaller, but I'd know you anywhere.

Albert: Arthur. *(Looks up at Arthur, delighted)*

Harold: *(bewildered)* Excuse me – shall I . . .

Albert: Harold. This is your brother.

Harold: Brother? I haven't got a brother.

Albert: Yes you have, son. Arthur.

Harold: Arthur?

Albert: Yeah. Arthur. He's your older brother.

Harold: Don't be daft. I'm an only child. I've always been an only child.

Albert: No, son. Arthur is your stepbrother.

Harold: Stepbrother? What do you mean, stepbrother?

Albert: Well, I met Arthur's mother before I met your mother.

Harold: I see. And?

Albert: Well, we were engaged for six years and then one night I couldn't control myself any longer. And then after that she went off me.

Harold: I'm not bloody well surprised.

Albert: Well, then Arthur came along, but she wouldn't marry me. She'd got in the cricket club. She said marriage and athletics didn't mix. Then she got picked for the women's cricket team to Australia – leg spinner, she was – and I never saw her again. Then I met your mother, and that was that.

Harold: Oh, what a nice story. Very savoury. How many more little bastards have you got spread around the world?

Albert: Don't talk to me like that.

Harold: Well, you certainly used to put yourself about a bit, didn't you? You never told me you had another son.

Albert: It was a long time ago. I haven't seen him since he was two years old. I didn't even know if he was still alive.

Arthur: Well, I am. Alive and kicking. So you're my kid brother?

Harold: *(coldly)* So it would appear.

Arthur: Well, this calls for a celebration.

3

Harold: Does it?

Arthur: Let's break open a few tubes of Foster's. I brought some with me, I'm told it's harder to find over here than an Arab at a bar mitzvah. They reckon your beer is flatter than a witch's tit. (*He opens one of the suitcases. It is full of cans of beer. He takes three out and hands one each to Harold and Albert*) There you go. (*Holds up his can in a toast*) Have a real drink. Well, here's to the Steptoe family. Long may it be reunited.

Albert: My two sons. Come on, Harold, drink up.

Harold: Cheers.

Arthur: Cripes, I needed that. My mouth was as dry as a kangaroo's jock strap.

Albert: There's so much to ask you, Arthur. First things first – where are you staying?

Arthur: Well, Pop, I'll tell you. I haven't as yet made any arrangements. I've only just fallen out the flaming aeroplane. I understand there's a million flop-houses up around Earls Court, so I suppose I shall have to make my way up there and . . .

Albert: No, no, son, you don't want to do that.

Harold: Why not?

Albert: You can stay here with us.

Harold: We haven't got any room.

Albert: Of course we have. We'll make room. You wouldn't want your brother living with strangers. He's just arrived from Australia. You can have Harold's room.

Harold: Wait a minute—

Albert: Harold can make up a bed down here for the time being.

Harold: Down here?

Arthur: That's very decent of you, Harold. I'm obliged to you.

Harold: Yes, but—

Arthur: Well, that's settled then. (*He opens another can of beer*) Very nice. I must say it's good to be back in the old country . . . in the bosom of my family. I can't tell you what it's like, Dad, to come home . . . and meet you again, and young Harold. Fine boy. Yes, a man needs roots.

Harold: Roots? You're not staying, are you – I mean, long? It's a holiday?

Arthur: Well, I don't know, young Harold. I'm thinking of staying here for good, now. I've been around a bit, you know. Done everything. Walkabout, sheep shearing, cattle droving, gold mining, pearl fishing . . .

Albert: Oh, how marvellous.

Harold: Yeah, it sounds much better than it is here. Bingo and telly, that's all we've got. You'll be bored to tears here. Especially when the rainy season starts.

Arthur: Rain? Love it. When you've spent seven years in the outback without seeing a drop, you've got no idea how beautiful rain is. No, I'm getting a bit long in the tooth now for gallivanting, I think it's time for me to settle down – and where better than in good old Pommieland, with your old dad and your kid brother?

(The taxi driver knocks on the door and comes in)

Driver: Excuse me, how much longer are you keeping my taxi out there?

Arthur: Stone the flaming crows, I forgot all about you.

Driver: Five pound ten, please.

Arthur: Five pound ten?

Driver: I turned the clock off when you got out.

Arthur: Maybe you did, but I think you turned the bastard on when I left Melbourne.

Driver: It's five pound ten.

Arthur: Just to come from London Airport? I'm not flaming daft, you know.

Driver: It's still five pound ten.

Arthur: Five pounds ten. *(Picks up his jacket and feels for some money)* Er . . . Harold, I don't seem to have any pommie money on me. I wonder if you'd mind paying Ned Kelly here for me.

Harold: What, five pound ten?

Albert: Pay the man, Harold. Arthur will give it back to you.

Arthur: Too right. Just as soon as I've changed my traveller's cheques.

Albert: Yeah. Of course he will.

(Harold gives the driver the money. The driver leaves)

Albert: It's marvellous to have you here, Arthur. Er . . . how's your mother?

Arthur: It's very sad. I'm sorry to say, the poor old lady passed on last month.

Albert: Oh dear. I'm very sorry.

Arthur: Yeah, a bit of a shock really, she'd never been crook in her life. Active right up till the last.

Albert: What happened to her?

Arthur: She keeled over with a half-shaved Merino ram between her legs. New South Wales Shearing Championships. She would have won, too. Thirty-nine seconds and she only had the back legs left. A great tragedy. A year's supply of Swan Lager, she was on. Not that it would have lasted her long, you understand. Do you want another?

Albert: Yeah, thanks. *(Takes beer)* Did she ever marry?

Arthur: No, not her. She shacked up with some Eyetie plonk grower when I was seven. But he used to beat the bejesus out of her and finally one night when he come home a bit Adrian Quist, she smashed him across the scone with a quart jar of his vino redo. She loaded up the Ford and we didn't stop for three hundred miles.

Harold: My mother was a schoolteacher. A very lovely woman. Very gentle. A lady she was, my mother. I don't believe a drop of alcohol ever passed her lips, did it, Father?

Albert: No, no, not your mother. Salvation Army, she was.

Harold: Yes, that's right. A very pious lady.

Arthur: Yeah? Funny how a feller can have two Sheilas so different, isn't it?

Harold: Yes. Very amusing.

Albert: Well, now you've come home, Arthur, we ought to start making plans for the future.

Harold: What plans?

Albert: Well, I mean, he's going to stay with us, he's got to start thinking about work, hasn't he?

Arthur: Work?

Harold: Yes, what a good idea. I'll take you down the Labour Exchange first thing in the morning. They're digging a new Tube tunnel, and I know they do use a lot of Commonwealth labour.

Arthur: Well now, wait a minute – I didn't come twelve thousand miles to dig my way across London.

Harold: Oh, I'm sorry, perhaps you have a trade? A profession?

Albert: Well, no, not exactly.

Harold: No.

Albert: Neither have you.

Harold: I'm different. I don't need one. I have my own business.

Albert: It's the family business. And Arthur's family. He can come in with us.

Harold: What?

Albert: You're always moaning about how hard you have to work. Arthur can take some of the load off you. I'll make him a partner.

Arthur: That is a very handsome offer, which I am delighted to accept.

Harold: Wait a minute. I have sweated my guts out building up this business, and I am not going to stand by and watch a perfect stranger walk in here and—

Albert: He is not a perfect stranger.

Harold: He is to me.

Albert: Well, he isn't to me. He is my son. My **eldest** son.

(This stops Harold in his tracks. He and Albert glare at each other. Harold turns and walks out of the room. Albert starts after him, but Arthur stops him)

Arthur: Leave him be, Pop. He'll be all right. It must be a shock to the young feller, me just turning up out of the blue. He's bound to be a bit jealous.

Albert: I can't understand it. After all I've done for him.

Arthur: He'll get over it. Give him time. Well, I'm going up to my room to clean up. I'll just pop outside first and point Percy at the porcelain. As it's my first day home, I'm going to take you and the young feller up to town and I'm going to buy you both some slap-up tucker in a bonza Frog caff.

Albert: Oh, that'll be marvellous.

Arthur: There's just one thing. I wonder if you could see your way clear to lending me a few quid – just till I cash my traveller's cheques, you understand . . .

Albert: Of course, son . . . anything you want. *(Gives him some money)* Five–ten?

Arthur: Better make it twenty . . . No, I'll tell you what *(looks at the notes in Albert's hand)*, make it a round fifty. Then I won't have to keep coming back to you.

Albert: Fifty it is. *(Gives money to Arthur)* It's so good to see you again, son. You don't know what this means to me, having both my sons around me. You've made an old man very happy.

Arthur: Yeah, well, it's great to be home again. *(Picks up his open case)* Oh, by the way, I've got a little present for you. *(He hands Albert a boomerang. Albert beams)*

SCENE 6
The yard. The gates are open. Albert is painting an 'S' on the end of 'SON'. Harold comes out of the house, walks to cart. He walks over to join Albert. He watches him painting.

Harold: So it's official now, is it? He's rowed himself in.

Albert: He has agreed to join the firm, yes.

Harold: I don't suppose he needed much persuading.

Albert: Harold, I can't understand why you're taking this attitude. Why do you resent him? He's your brother.

Harold: How do you know? How can you be sure? A middle-aged out-of-work Australian turns up, you've never seen him before – he could be anybody. He says he's your son and you believe him. You're so gullible.

Albert: He's my son all right. All the photographs he's shown me – him and his mother – the things he's told me – he couldn't know all that if he wasn't. Oh yes, he's my son all right. He's got my ears. And my nose.

Harold: And your money. Where is he now?

Albert: He's in bed. I just took his breakfast up.

Harold: See? You've never brought me breakfast in bed in my life. It makes me sick the way you run round after him.

Albert: I don't run round after him.

Harold: Well, get him up. If he's a partner he's got to do his full share.

Albert: He can't get up, he's not well. It's our weather, it's playing his war wound up.

Harold: Oh, he's got a war wound as well, has he? It runs in the family, don't it? Nobody can do any work except me.

Albert: He was a prisoner of war of the Japanese.

Harold: And I bet they were bleeding glad to get rid of him. He certainly hasn't seen the rising sun since he's been here.

Albert: You're very bitter, Harold. This isn't like you.

Harold: It is like me. You just don't know me, do you? Forty years you've had me. Four days you've had him. And you know him better than you do me. Sitting up all night yarning with him and laughing with him. I've heard you. And buying him drinks. That's another thing. He's soon got used to our rotten beer, hasn't he? Yes, I'm bitter. I'm resentful. I'm jealous. I'm all those things. I think it's diabolical that a man can work as hard as I do, and see it given away like this. To someone who hasn't put a thing into the firm.

Albert: Well, that's where you're wrong. He has. He's put his shares up in lieu of capital.

Harold: Shares? What shares?

Albert: He invested all his money in an Australian nickel mine. You've heard of Poseidon?

Harold: He's got shares in that?

Albert: No. The one next door to it. The Poseidon reef goes right under his land.

Harold: Oh, my gawd.

Albert: He's got the lot there. Nickel, gold, opals, tin, steel.

Harold: Bread pudding, marmalade. You daft pillock! You can't have steel mines, you **make** steel. You'd believe anything, wouldn't you?

Albert: And it's better than Poseidon. All his stuff is right on the surface, he doesn't have to dig for it. He's got oil as well.

Harold: Naturally.

Albert: Right there on top. He reckons if you walk across his land in a pair of golf shoes, you leave a trail of little gushers behind you.

Harold: And you believe all this?

Albert: Of course I do. He told me.

Harold: Dad, he's a con man. He's a ponce.

Albert: You don't like him, do you?

Harold: No, I don't. He never gave me a boomerang. It sickens me to see the way you've been taken in by him. You haven't got any time for me any more.

Albert: That's not true.

Harold: It is true. You think the sun shines out of his earholes. I don't exist any more as far as you're concerned.

Albert: It's natural for a man to have a deep affection for his first-born.

Harold: I see. You favour him if you want to. But I'm warning you. I'm not going to stand by and see everything I've worked for handed on a plate to one of your illegitimate sprogs.

Albert: There's enough for all of us.

Harold: Where – show me where. But how many more are going to turn up once the word gets round?

Albert: None. There's just you and Arthur.

Harold: That you know of. The way you moved around, gawd knows how many there are. All the birds you used to have in your young days – you're a one-man population explosion. I bet you've sired more bleeding offspring than an Aberdeen Angus. You ought to be on a stud farm, with a big rosette stuck behind your earhole. And you'd have them all in the firm, wouldn't you? We'll finish up with a bigger board than ICI.

Albert: We won't. There'll just be the three of us. You're being very childish. Arthur is just the sort of man we need in this firm. We've never had a good financial brain running the business.

Harold: Thank you very much. I've managed perfectly well up to now.

Albert: Arthur says our books are in a shocking state.

Harold: Oh, you've shown him the books? You had no right. I don't want any Tom, Dick or Harry knowing how much director's fees I've been voted.

Albert: Well, he says the first thing he wants to do is change our in and out column.

Harold: I bet he does. I put it all in, and he takes it all out.

Albert: He knows what he's talking about, does Arthur.

Harold: And I don't.

Albert: I'm not blaming you. You do the best you can. It's just that Arthur's more . . . er . . . well, he's had a much better education than you have.

Harold: Everybody's had a better education than me. I used to spend more time on the horse and cart than I did at school.

Albert: You didn't like school. You were always hopping the wag.

Harold: That's no reason for not sending me. You should have made me go.

Albert: I couldn't, you were too big. You were heavier than me when you was eleven. I tried to make you go to school, but you kept threatening to wallop me.

Harold: Wallop you? When I was eleven?

Albert: Yeah. I was frightened of you. I couldn't control you. I tried to get you into Borstal but they wouldn't have you.

Harold: Oh, thank you very much. What an idyllic childhood I had.

Albert: It's true.

Harold: It's not true. I never had a chance. The number of times you said 'It's a nice day today, you don't want to go to school, come out with me on the round and get some fresh air.' No wonder I couldn't keep up.

Albert: You never used to mind.

Harold: Of course I didn't. I was so far behind at school it was humiliating. Three years running I was kept back. I was the only bloke in the juniors who wore long trousers. If I hadn't gone in the Army I still wouldn't be able to read and write. You crippled my mind, you did. And now you're holding it against me. I could have been a doctor or a bandleader or something. I always liked music. You never helped me in that, either, did you? That teacher said I was musically inclined and you ought to encourage me. But you wouldn't buy me a piano, would you? You taught me to whistle instead.

Albert: I got you that piano off the round.

Harold: There were thirty-two notes missing. I couldn't even play chopsticks. And the lid kept falling down on my fingers. A version therapy they call that today. No, mate, I never stood a chance.

Albert: You can't blame me for your own shortcomings. I'm Arthur's father as well, and he's done all right.

Harold: Only because he got away from you. I wish it had been the other way round. I wish I'd been the illegitimate one. I wish I'd been taken away from you. I might have amounted to something then. I would have turned out a bloody sight better than he has.

(*A pause*)

Albert: I never knew you wanted to be a bandleader.

Harold: You never bothered to find out, did you? You just weren't interested. That's what I can't forgive. You were more concerned with yourself than with my future. And now what little I've managed to build up for myself you expect me to share with him. Well, I'm sorry, Dad, it's not on. You're going to have to choose. Me or him.

Albert: That's not fair. You can't ask a man to choose between his sons. Not just like that.

Harold: Yes, you can. It's very simple. Either he goes or I go. Make up your mind.

Albert: I can't, Harold.

Harold: Right then, I'm off.

Albert: Harold . . .

Harold: I'm sorry. That's the way it is. I would have gone before but I've always had to look after you. Well, that's changed now. It's his turn. I've had you for forty years, now he can have a go. And good luck to you.

Albert: But what about the business?

Harold: Let him run it. If you can get him up, that is.

Albert: Don't go, Harold. Not now. It's time to go out on the round.

Harold: I have completed my last round for this firm.

Albert: But who's going to do it?

Harold: May I suggest you go into the house and turf Wallaby Jim of the Islands out of bed. Give him a map, put him on the cart, and let him get on with it.

Albert: He won't be able to drive that horse, you know she won't go out with anyone else but you. Nobody else can handle her.

Harold: Then I suggest he sells off a few of his nickel shares and buys himself a kangaroo. I'm sure he'll be at home with one of them. He'll be able to hop around in no time. I'm going to start up on my own. (*He walks off. He takes the paintbrush and paints out the new 'S' in the sign on the gates*)

Albert: No, Harold.

Harold: Goodbye. (*He leaves*)

Albert: Come back, Harold. I need you, Harold.

(*Albert walks sadly back into the house*)

SCENE 7
The hall. Arthur comes downstairs in his dressing gown.

Arthur: Good morning, Dad.

Albert: Afternoon.

Arthur: *(winces)* The old war wound's still playing me up, Dad. I know how you must feel now. Still, perhaps in a few days I might be able to start giving you a bit of a hand round the station.

Albert: It's about time.

Arthur: Well, I've been going through the books, I haven't just been lying up there scratching me kaboona. I've got one or two ideas. I notice we allow young Harold ten shillings a day for his lunch. Now, if we give him sandwiches that will be a net saving of—

Albert: He's gone.

Arthur: Gone – gone where?

Albert: He walked out.

Arthur: Oh, that's a blow. Still, he'll be back when his old guts start rumbling. In the meantime, I wonder if you could lend me another fiver? There's a horse running at Kempton Park this afternoon . . .

Albert: Yeah, well, there's one in the stables raring to go as well. Get your clothes on. *(He goes into the lounge)*
(Arthur reacts)

SCENE 8
A street. Harold is pushing a handcart along. He has a board announcing 'Harold Steptoe & Co' nailed to the cart. He is very dejected. A woman standing by her gate beckons to him. He pushes the cart towards her hopefully. She hands him a pullover full of holes. Harold is disgusted. He hands her a few coppers and goes wearily on his way.

Albert is watching him from a corner.

A little later, Harold is walking dejectedly down a very slummy street. All the houses are extremely dilapidated. Harold goes up to one of them and lets himself in the front door.

SCENE 9
Inside the dingy house. Harold makes his way along the top landing and goes into a tiny, terribly dilapidated, sparsely furnished

and very depressing room. Albert is sitting in the one chair in the room, huddled close to an old gas fire in the fireplace.

Albert: Hallo, son.

Harold: What are you doing here?

Albert: I've been looking for you for three weeks now.

Harold: Oh yes?

Albert: Lenny Jenkins told me where you were living. Your landlady let me in.

(Harold looks at the fire. Albert follows his glance)

Albert: I put a shilling in.

Harold: Oh. There was no need, thank you very much. I'm quite capable of providing my own heating. *(He moves over to warm his hands and the fire goes out with a 'pop'. He fishes in his pocket but hasn't got any money. Albert takes a shilling out and puts it in the meter and lights the gas again. Harold warms his hands, then stands with his back to the fire)* Well ... what brings you to this neck of the woods?

Albert: I was worried about you. I hadn't heard from you, and I was wondering how you were getting along.

Harold: Oh, I'm very well, thank you. I'm doing nicely.

Albert: *(looking round the room)* You're going to stay here then, are you?

Harold: Oh, good heavens no, this is just temporary accommodation until I find something more suitable. I've seen quite a nice little mews cottage that I'm thinking of renting. *(He goes to the table. There is a half-used wrapped loaf, a half-empty bottle of milk, and a half-eaten half-pound of butter still in the wrapper. Harold takes a slice of bread, sticks it on a fork, sits on the dishevelled, unmade bed and starts to toast the bread. He coughs slightly)*

Albert: You're doing well, then?

Harold: Oh yes, I can't complain. The business is coming along very nicely.

Albert: You got yourself a horse and cart, then.

Harold: Oh yes, I'm very pleased with it. Four-year-old horse. Seventeen hands, beautiful animal. I'm particularly pleased with the cart. It's brand new, bigger than your own of course, but then I had to have it to handle the volume of trade I'm doing.

Albert: Oh, good.

(There is a pause. Harold coughs again. He takes his toast and butters it)

Albert: Aren't you going to put any jam on it? You always eat it with jam on it.

Harold: I haven't got any . . . I'm on a diet. I've given up jam. Businessmen eat far too much. Digging their graves with their own teeth, as my specialist put it.

Albert: Harold.

Harold: Yes?

Albert: Come back, Harold. Please.

Harold: I think we have had all that out. I don't see the advantage of discussing it any further.

Albert: I need you, Harold. The business needs you.

Harold: I'm sure your new managing director can look after the business.

Albert: He's gone.

Harold: Gone? Gone where?

Albert: He's hopped it. Gone back to Australia, I think. You were right, Harold, he was a ponce. A lazy no-good con man.

Harold: I told you he was. A bloke like him wouldn't take the horse and cart out.

Albert: Oh, he took it out all right. The only trouble was, he didn't bring it back. He flogged it. I haven't seen him since.

Harold: The swine. Well, what did you expect? They're not all like me.

Albert: I don't know what to do. I haven't even got a horse and cart now. Come back Harold. I can't manage on my own.

Harold: I don't know . . . I'd like to help you, I really would, but it's going to be very difficult. There's a yard full of people relying on me . . .

Albert: I realize I couldn't ask you to close down just like that. I thought we could make it on a proper business footing. A merger. Between your firm and mine. We'll call it Steptoe & Steptoe.

Harold: You mean a reverse take-over.

Albert: Do I?

Harold: Yes. It's quite a common arrangement when a smaller firm like mine appears to merge with a larger firm but in effect takes it over. Yes, interesting, I must admit. I suppose we could enter into exploratory dialogue. The assets of the two companies would have to be fully analysed as to . . . *(The gas fire goes out with a 'pop')*

Albert: That didn't last long. She's got that well rigged. *(Feels in his pocket)* I haven't got any more shillings.

Harold: Oh. I've only got notes.

Albert: Look, I tell you what, Harold, let's carry on the exploratory dialogue round home. The fire's on. I banked it up before I came out.

Harold: *(rubbing his hands from the cold)* Well, of course, psychologically I'd be at a disadvantage talking on your home ground.

Albert: I've got a steak and kidney pudding in the oven.

Harold: Have you? *(Licks his lips involuntarily)*

Albert: And a sherry trifle. And an upside-down cake.

Harold: Yeah.

Albert: And I've got some jam as well.

Harold: Well . . . I suppose the venue of the talks doesn't really have any bearing on the eventual outcome. Yes, all right, I'll concede the point.

Albert: Good. Shall we go now?

Harold: These are just exploratory talks . . .

Albert: Yeah, of course.

Harold: Come on, then. *(He goes out of room)*

(Albert notices the rent book on the mantelpiece. He takes it and looks in it. He nods to himself, then goes out)

SCENE 10

The street. Harold and Albert come out of the house. They walk around the corner. Albert comes back on his own and goes up to the front door. The door is opened by the coloured landlady. Albert opens the rent book, lays two fivers on it and hands it to her.

Harold appears and waves for the old man to hurry up. Albert hurries over to rejoin him. As they walk off together they are passed by a horse and cart. Harold and Albert recognize it as theirs. They turn and run after it as it goes down the street.

Men Of Letters

First transmission 21 February 1972

Men Of Letters featured
Anthony Sharp as The Vicar
and was produced by John Howard Davies

SCENE 1
The Steptoes' lounge. Harold and Albert are engrossed in a game of Scrabble. Harold is surveying the board closely. He examines the letters he has on his rack. Albert tries to see what letters Harold has. Harold shields them with his arm. The game is three-quarters finished, the board filled with words. Harold tries to work out some possible goes. He finally gives up.

Harold: I can't go.

Albert: I can.

Harold: Well, all right then, go. Don't sit there gloating. Put your word down.

(Albert puts two letters on the board on the end of a word already down, thus making a three-letter word)

Harold: What's that, what's that?

Albert: B ... U ... M – BUM. That's three – four – five – six – seven. Triple letter score, double word score, that's sixteen, and fourteen, thirty.

(Albert writes down his score. He takes two letters from the pool to make up his rack to the allowed seven letters)

Harold: What a filthy mind you've got.

Albert: What's wrong with that?

Harold: It's vulgar, that's what's wrong with it. Honestly, this is supposed to be an erudite game to increase one's word power. Look at that board. It's disgusting. There's not one word you've put down that can be used in decent company. Not one word more than four letters – that board is nothing less than a display of unadulterated filth.

Albert: They still count though, don't they?

Harold: They don't.

Albert: They do. If they're in the dictionary, they count. And bum's in the dictionary. It's your go.

Harold: I'm not sure that bum is in the dictionary. You don't think all them professors up at Oxford would waste their time discussing the merits and meanings of the word 'bum'. They wouldn't use dirty words like that.

Albert: My bum's not dirty. What I mean is, my bum is the American word for a tramp.

Harold: Ah well, that's where I've got you. You are not allowed to use colloquialisms or slang.

Albert: In that case I stand by the English bum. That being the part of the anatomy that swells out the back of your trousers. It's your go.

Harold: Oh, this is ridiculous. I can't compete with this sort of thing. If I'd thought this game was going to degenerate into a mere catalogue of crudities, I wouldn't have started it in the first place.

Albert: You're just narked because I'm winning.

Harold: Well, of course, if you don't care what sort of words you use, that's not difficult. Look at the difference between the quality of my words and your words. At least I'm having a go at keeping the tone up.

Albert: You're not winning though, are you? That's what it's all about, mate. Have you got an S?

Harold: Supposing I have?

Albert: You could stick it on the end of my bum and make it bums.

Harold: I'd rather not if you don't mind. (*He re-examines the board. He finally decides*) Well . . . at least I can clean your word up. (*He adds two letters to 'bum'*) B . . . U . . . M – BUM. Your word. B . . . U . . . M . . . P . . . S – BUMPS. My word. Three and one, and a triple letter score, makes seven. (*He writes down his score and takes two letters from the pool*)

Albert: Bumps – that's nice. That S lets me in lovely. (*He puts two letters under the S*) S . . . O . . . D – SOD. Triple letters, three . . . O, one . . . D, two. Six altogether. (*He writes down his score. Takes two letters from the pool*)

Harold: I am not allowing sod.

Albert: Why not? A piece of turf, nothing wrong with that. Shakespeare uses it.

Harold: I don't care if Barbara Cartland uses it. That's not the way you meant it. You meant it as a swear word. You always mean them as swear words, because you're dirty and crude and horrible.

Albert: Your go.

Harold: I can't go.

Albert: I can see one.

Harold: I'm not interested.

Albert: Have you got a blank?

Harold: I'm not telling you.

Albert: Use that as a K, then if you've got an . . .

Harold: No. I will not stoop to using obscenities. Besides, you've already used it.

Albert: So you can't go, then.

Harold: I didn't say that, did I. I think I shall change all my letters.

Albert: You can't. There's only four left.

Harold: All right then, I'll change three of them. (*He exchanges three of the letters in his rack for the three letters in the pool. He puts his new letters in his rack. They consist of Q, Z, T, J, W, G, X*)

Harold: Hmm. I suppose if we were Polish I might be able to have a stab. Let's see. Quizt. Jwgx.

Albert: You can't go, can you?

Harold: No, I can't.

Albert: I can. C . . . R . . . U . . . M . . . (*He puts the letters on the board*)

Harold: What's that?

Albert: Crum.

Harold: Crum?

Albert: Yeah. What you get in bed when you've been eating biscuits.

Harold: You don't spell it like that.

Albert: Don't you?

Harold: There's a B on the end of it.

Albert: Is there?

Harold: No wonder you only put filthy words down, they're the only ones you can spell. My go.

Albert: No, it's not. I can still go. What's that word you put down there?

Harold: (*looks on board*) Pet.

(*Albert puts the C . . . R . . . U . . . M in front of the P . . . E . . . T*)

Albert: There you are, C . . . R . . . U . . . M . . . P . . . E . . . T – CRUMPET. Which you also get in bed. That's three, four, five, and three's eight, and three's eleven, twelve, thirteen. A triple letter and a double word score. Twenty-nine altogether. *(He writes down his score)* That's five hundred and twenty-three to me and fifty-six to you. *(He takes the remaining letters from the pool and puts them back in his rack)*

Harold: Well, you won't make anything out of the two Ks and an N I just threw away.

(Albert puts all his letters onto the board)

Albert: Da de da de da de da . . . KNICKERS. I'm out. That's fifty points for using all my letters. That's five hundred and thirty-five I've won by, at a penny a point, that's five pounds thirty-five you owe me. *(Harold turns away)* Do you want to play another game?

Harold: No.

Albert: It's a good game, ain't it?

Harold: It is when it's played properly, but not when it's played by dirty old men like you.

(There is a knock on the front door)

Albert: Who's that?

Harold: Stone me, every time there's a knock at the door you say 'Who's that?' It's a very annoying habit. How do I know who it is – I haven't got X-ray eyes. I shall go out and open the door, and if it's got anything remotely to do with you I shall tell you who it is.

(More knocking on the door)

Albert: If you don't go and answer it neither of us will know who it is.

(More knocking – Harold exits to hall)

SCENE 2
The hall. Harold walks to the front door. There is more knocking.

Harold: *(walking to the front door)* All right, all right, don't knock the bleeding house down. *(He opens the door. The vicar is standing there)* Oh. Hello, Vicar.

Vicar: Good evening, Mr Steptoe. Inclement weather, is it not?

Harold: Oh yes, most inclement, yes.

Vicar: It is on nights like this that one's thoughts go out to our sailors and fishermen.

Harold: Yes indeed, it must be very umpty out there. I wouldn't fancy it.

Vicar: Nor I. Indeed no.

Harold: It's funny, ain't it, we all take a bit of fish for granted, don't we?

Vicar: We do, we do, yes indeed we do.

Harold: Yes.

Vicar: Hardly a thought do we spare for those brave souls.

Harold: Quite, quite. *(Pause)* How much do you want?

Vicar: Pardon?

Harold: I . . . I thought you were collecting.

Vicar: Oh, goodness me, no.

Harold: Oh, well, you'd better come in, then.

Vicar: Thank you, you're most kind.

> *(The vicar comes in, Harold slams the door and takes the vicar's coat)*

Albert: *(shouting, off)* Who was it?

Harold: The vicar.

Albert: Oh gawd, is he on the ear'ole again?

Harold: *(laughing in embarrassment)* My father, he knows you're here, it's just a joke. *(The vicar laughs, also in embarrassment)* This way.

SCENE 3

The lounge. Albert is pouring himself a drink as Harold shows the vicar in, and doesn't immediately see the visitor.

Albert: He's already had two bob out of me this year. He must think we're made of . . .

Harold: Father.

> *(Harold coughs. Albert turns and sees the vicar)*

Albert: *(mutters)* Oh gawd. Hello, Vicar. I didn't recognize you with your clothes on . . . your suit, I mean, I – er – it's a nice one, isn't it, it's not one of ours, is it?

Vicar: I beg your pardon?

Albert: You didn't get it out of that sackful we gave you for Bangladesh?

Harold: Father, the vicar is hardly likely to nick clothes intended for refugees.

Albert: I didn't mean anything. I wouldn't blame him if he had – his needs are as great as theirs, he hasn't got much has he, I mean . . .

Harold: Father, would you like to go and make a cup of tea? It's rather inclement out.

Albert: Tea? He don't want tea, do you, Vicar? Have something to keep the cold out . . . (*He pours a Scotch from the optics*) Here you are, a nice drop of gold watch.

Vicar: Thank you very much.

Albert: God bless you and the devil miss you.

(*Albert drinks his in one gulp, the vicar sips his and shudders slightly*)

Harold: Don't give me one, will you? Would you care to sit down, Vicar?

Vicar: Thank you.

(*He goes to sit at the table and sees the Scrabble board*)

Vicar: Oh, Scrabble. My favourite game. You've just finished I see. (*He puts his glasses on to look at the board*)

(*Harold reacts in alarm and quickly mixes the letters up*)

Harold: It's not a very high standard, we haven't got the command of words like what you have.

Vicar: Perhaps you'd both like to come round to the vicarage one evening, my wife is a very keen player. We could make a foursome up.

Albert: Oh yeah, I'd like that.

Harold: Er, no, I don't think that's a very good idea. You'd be much too good for us. You'd crucify us – I mean, that is . . . how's your knees?

Vicar: Greatly improved, thank you.

Harold: The vicar had a touch of housemaid's knee, Father.

Albert: Oh, I am sorry.

Vicar: Yes, an occupational hazard, I'm afraid, one has to do a great deal of kneeling in my game.

Albert: You want to get your missus to sew pads inside your trousers. She wants to use one of her padded bras, cut in half and strap them round your knees. They fit lovely. I knew a carpet layer who swore by them and he reckons . . .

Harold: Father, I'm sure the vicar can make his own medical arrangements, without laying himself open to a charge of transvestism. Why don't you go and put the blanket over the horse? And then go to bed.

Albert: No, I want to talk to the vicar.

Harold: Then kindly moderate your language. (*To vicar*) Um . . . to what do we owe the pleasure of this visit? I mean, if it's about me not coming to church, I do believe I have made my position clear to you in the past. While I have nothing against you, intellectually I am like Bertrand Russell before me, a Humanist . . . and consequently I find myself unable to subscribe to the Christian ethos and dogma.

Vicar: Yes, yes, I remember our conversation that evening very well. Very cogently reasoned, I thought. I remember your argument that Pascal and Calvin were . . . er . . . berks, I believe you said, made a great impression on my wife.

Harold: Did I say that? I'm dreadfully sorry.

Vicar: Not at all, one often gets carried away in a theological discussion.

Harold: Yes, but I shouldn't have used language like that. If you could explain that I was a bit het up, and your hospitality was on the generous side and I was a wee bit Brahms and Liszt.

Vicar: Brahms and Liszt. I shall tell her. No, Mr Steptoe, the reason for my visit is quite different. Frankly, I have come to ask a favour of you.

Harold: Anything. Please don't hesitate to ask.

Vicar: As you may know, this week we are celebrating the centenary of our church.

Harold: Get away.

Vicar: Yes, one hundred years of bringing the good word to the people of Shepherd's Bush – yes, a great deal has changed since then.

Albert: Yeah, you're getting a lot of competition from the Moslems now, ain't you?

Harold: Father!

Albert: Well, it's true. They were pouring out of that converted cinema last week. Looked just like a bus garage, it did.

Vicar: I don't regard it as competition. All the great religions of the world are there for the glory of God. In my Father's house there are many mansions.

Albert: Are there? Well, I wish he'd put a few round here. The living conditions are diabolical.

Vicar: Yes, I am cognizant of the problem. However . . .

Harold: Yes, go on, vicar.

Vicar: We have decided to publish a special enlarged edition of the Parish Magazine.

Harold: What a good idea.

Vicar: And I shall need all the contributions I can get.

Albert: *(puts his hand in his pocket)* I thought so. How much do you want?

Vicar: No, no, I mean articles . . . articles for inclusion. My wife thought it would be rather nice if we had articles about some of the more exotic trades and professions carried out in the Parish throughout the years.

Albert: We've had some of those round here. Next door there used to be a right old knocking shop.

Harold: Yes – we got a lot of noise from there. It used to be a wheelwright.

Vicar: And as you are one of the oldest established firms in the area we wondered whether one of you would care to write about the history of rag and boning in Shepherd's Bush.

Harold: Oh, I should be delighted to.

Albert: So would I.

Harold: Father, I think I'd better write it.

Albert: I know more about it than you do.

Harold: No, you don't. And you can't write as well as I can, either. I was always top of the class at composition, you know that. I always got nine out of ten and I got a star once. Oh yes, words have always been my strong point. You leave it to me, Vicar.

Albert: I want to do it.

Harold: Well, you can't. You'll have to do something else, won't you?

Albert: I want to do the article.

Harold: Well, you're not going to do the article. I'm the artistic one in this house.

Albert: Cobblers, you can't even spell.

Harold: Who can't?

Albert: You can't.

Harold: I can spell better than you can.

Albert: Who can?

Harold: I can.

Albert: Oh no you can't.

Harold: Oh yes I can.

Albert: All right then, spell chrysanthemum.

Harold: C . . . H . . . R . . . I . . . S . . . T . . . – er – C . . . R . . . I . . . – um – K . . . H . . . R . . . I am hardly likely to use the word 'chrysanthemum' in an article about rag and boning.

Albert: That's where you're wrong, because Charlie Harris's horse is called Chrysanthemum.

Harold: I don't care, I won't mention him.

Albert: You can't write an article about rag and boning without mentioning Charlie Harris. He'd be furious. His family have been in it even longer than ours.

Harold: Then I shall say Charlie Harris and his horse.

Albert: Because you can't spell Chrysanthemum.

    (They are gradually raising their voices)

Harold: I can look it up in the dictionary.

Albert: How can you look it up when you can't spell it?

Harold: I'll get somebody to spell it for me **then** I'll look it up.

Albert: How do you spell 'Mullable'?

Harold: I'm not interested in spelling mullable.

Albert: That's Bottles Ferrari's horse.

Harold: I don't give a toss whose horse it is.

Albert: How many horses and carts followed Arthur Philpotts' coffin in 1928?

Harold: Twenty-three.

Albert: Thirty-six. You don't know nothing. You can't spell. You're not qualified. I've been a rag and bone man all my life.

Harold: So have I.

Albert: I was a rag and bone man before you were born.

Harold: And I'll be a rag and bone man after you're dead.

Albert: How do you know?

Harold: Because I'm going to kill you if you don't shut up.

Vicar: Why don't you both write it?

Harold: You keep out of this. Oh, I'm sorry, Vicar, I beg your pardon. I forgot you were here. No, it wouldn't work, I couldn't collaborate with him. One cannot undertake creative work with somebody who gets on your threepenny bits as much as he does.

Vicar: Well, this needs the judgement of Solomon.

Harold: You're going to chop him in half.

Vicar: Why don't you toss for it? *(Takes a coin out of his pocket)* You call, Mr Steptoe. *(Tosses the coin and holds it on the back of his hand)*

Albert: Heads.

Vicar: *(looks at coin)* Tails.

Harold: *(childishly triumphant)* Aha. You lost, you lost, you lost. I'm doing it. I'm doing it. *(Gives Albert the V sign three times quickly punctuated with three raspberries)*

Albert: *(scornfully)* You great big nellie. What are you? You want to get back in your cot, mate.

Vicar: Don't get upset, Mr Steptoe, we'd still like a contribution from you.

Albert: Would you?

Vicar: Of course.

Albert: Anything?

Vicar: Of course. Anything you like.

Albert: Right. You're on. I'll go and do it now. (*He goes to the door*)

Vicar: Goodnight, Mr Steptoe. Thank you for the drop of . . . er . . . gold watch.

Albert: Any time. (*He goes out*)

Harold: I'll see you out, Vicar.

SCENE 4
The hall. Harold helps the vicar on with coat.

Harold: Can I illustrate my article with photographs?

Vicar: Yes, that would be delightful.

Harold: I'm sure you'll be pleased with it.

Vicar: I'm sure I shall.

Harold: My teacher was always complimenting me on my literary style. I was thinking of taking up journalism when I left school, but old Miseryguts wouldn't let me. He wouldn't let me do anything. (*He opens the front door*)

Vicar: Goodnight, Mr Steptoe, I shall look forward to reading your article.

Harold: Goodnight, Vicar.

Vicar: (*looking up at the sky*) Ah yes, pity the poor sailors and fishermen.

Harold: Are they still out there?

Vicar: Goodnight, Mr Steptoe.

    (*He goes. Harold shuts the door*)

Harold: This could be the start of a new career . . .

SCENE 5
The lounge. Harold is at his desk, typing with one finger, painfully slowly. He is struggling. He crosses out a line. Finally he tears the sheet out, screws it up and throws it on the floor to join the pile of other screwed-up bits of paper. He puts another sheet in the machine. The table is cluttered with reference books, photographs, reels of tape recordings. Albert enters.

Harold: Oh, what a stupid place to put an R.

Albert: What's all this rubbish?

Harold: That's my research. Reference books, taped interviews, photographs. I've interviewed and photographed every totter within two miles. I don't mess about. When I do a thing I do it properly.

Albert: How much have you written?

Harold: Mind your own business.

(Albert looks over his shoulder)

Albert: You haven't started yet. Struggling a bit, are you?

Harold: It's all up here, don't worry. I know exactly what I'm going to write, it's just a question of getting it down. Flaubert had much the same trouble. He said every word was like tearing the flesh from his body. You go away and do yours.

Albert: I've done it.

Harold: Done it?

Albert: Last week.

Harold: What have you done?

Albert: Mind your own business.

Harold: Can't be much good if you did it that quickly. Probably extremely facile. Great work always takes a long time. *(He starts typing again with one finger. He puts another sheet in the machine and types the title again)* A . . . Hundred . . . Years . . . of . . . Totting . . . by Harold K. Steptoe.

Albert: It'll be a hundred and ten years by the time you've finished.

(Harold starts typing again)

Harold: The pale wintry sun shone down from an opalescent sky as the tired old carthorse . . .

(Albert switches the tape recorder on. We hear a totter talking)

Totter's voice: Yeah, well, in 1926 during the General Strike . . .

Albert: That's Charlie Harris.

Totter's voice: . . . under my Dad's leadership we organized a relief column to feed the Jarrow Marchers en route, so to speak.

Albert: Bleeding liar.

Harold: Turn that off. *(He switches the machine off)*

Albert: He's a liar, I tried to organize that. He wouldn't give you the drippings from his nose. What else did he tell you?

Harold: Oh, he gave me some marvellous material – wonderful human interest. About how when Charlie got married he had nowhere to live so he sent his old dad to the pictures and when his old dad got back all his furniture was out on the kerb, the door was locked, and Charlie made his dad live in the stable.

Albert: That's not true either. That was me and your grandfather. He's taking credit for everything. That article is going to be a tissue of lies.

Harold: All right then, I'll interview you. Get your side of it.

(Albert sits at the table. Harold switches on the tape recorder, holds the microphone up, looks at the volume dial)

Harold: Say something into that, get the level.

Albert: What shall I say?

Harold: Anything. What did you have for breakfast this morning?

Albert: Sausages, eggs and bacon.

Harold: Sausages?

Albert: Yeah.

(Harold switches the machine off)

Harold: You said there weren't any sausages.

Albert: Well, there weren't after I'd had them. There was only six, anyway.

Harold: Six? I could have had three of them. It's me who does the work, I'm entitled to go out of a morning with something inside me. You greedy, hungry-gutted, selfish little . . .

Albert: Are you going to interview me or not? I can't sit here all night arguing the toss with you. My time's valuable.

Harold: I'm cooking the breakfast tomorrow. Right. *(He switches the machine on. Into mike)*, One – two – three – testing, Mary had a little lamb, its fleece was white as snow. That's all right. A Hundred Years of Totting by Harold K. Steptoe. Interview number twenty-six, Albert Steptoe. *(Clears throat)* Mr Steptoe, what are your earliest recollections of the rag and bone business in Shepherd's Bush? *(He puts the microphone in front of the old man)*

Albert: I'm not telling you.

(Harold switches the machine off)

Harold: What's the point of having an interview if you're not going to say anything?

Albert: I'm not writing your article for you.

Harold: I'm not asking you. Gorblimey, Boswell could hardly have written his biography of Doctor Johnson if every time Boswell asked him something he'd said 'I'm not telling you'. Now then, we'll start again.

Albert: You just want to pick my brains.

Harold: I shall pick them straight out of your ears in a minute. Now then. *(He switches the machine on again. Each time one speaks Harold has to move the microphone backwards and forwards)*

Harold: Mr Steptoe, in your seventy years as a rag and bone man you must have seen many changes.

Albert: Yes, I have.

(Pause)

Harold: Well?

Albert: Well, what?

Harold: Well, what are they?

Albert: Oh. Well, we used to have trams on the roads in them days.

Harold: Yes?

Albert: Well, we haven't got them now.

(Harold puts his hand over the mike)

Harold: Are you trying to take the slash?

Albert: No.

Harold: Well, get on with it, then. *(Takes hand off the mike)* It must have been difficult to drive a horse and cart in those days.

Albert: Oh, it was. Dangerous as well. I remember once having a heavy load on and I got my wheels caught in the tramlines at Marble Arch, and I had to go all the way back to Putney depot before I could turn round.

Harold: Couldn't they have put a No 6 on the horse's backside and switched the points and sent you to Shepherd's Bush?

Albert: Are you calling me a liar?

Harold: Yes, and if you don't take it seriously I shall switch this machine off and fetch you a knuckle sandwich right up your bracket. All right? Tell me, Mr Steptoe, bearing in mind that this article is for the Church Magazine, so that we won't want any filth – and I realize that's placing an unfair handicap on you – can you think of any interesting incidents in your long career as a rag and bone man?

Albert: Yes. When I was seven, my dad bought me a homing pigeon.

Harold: Oh, that's nice.

Albert: And when we were hard up, I had to go down the market and sell it. For a tanner.

Harold: Oh, that's very sad.

Albert: I sold the pigeon five hundred and twenty-three times before we were tumbled.

(They both laugh)

Harold: That's marvellous, that's the sort of stuff I want. Got any more like that?

Albert: Oh yeah. I remember during the Depression I was totting down the Goldhawk Road, it was pouring with snow and this woman comes out and she calls me in . . .

SCENE 6

The lounge. Harold is typing away as fast as he can. He is delighted with what he is writing. An Anglepoise light is shining on to the typewriter. Harold is wearing an eyeshade and armbands. He pours himself a slug of whisky and drinks it, then continues typing. He finishes with a flourish, tears the paper out of the machine.

SCENE 7
The vicarage hall, where the vicar is on the phone.

Vicar: I've just finished reading your article, Mr Steptoe, and it really is first class. Absolutely fascinating. Just what we wanted. No, I don't intend cutting it at all. I don't pretend to understand all the colloquialisms but I'm sure the parishioners will. Yes, we're going to press today. Five thousand copies.

SCENE 8
The Steptoes' lounge. Albert is playing Scrabble with himself. He makes a word, then goes to the other side of the table and makes a word with the other set of letters. Harold enters carrying a copy of the Parish Magazine.

Albert: Oh, hello. Ooh, is that the Parish Magazine?
Harold: It is.
Albert: Are our bits in there?
Harold: They are.
Albert: Let's have a look. I've been trying to get one everywhere.
Harold: So have lots of people.
Albert: They've sold out, have they?
Harold: No. They've been impounded by the police. One hour after the first five hundred copies were distributed the vicarage was raided and the vicar was arrested on a charge of publishing obscene literature calculated to corrupt public morals. I take it your contribution was the crossword puzzle?
Albert: That's right. There was nothing wrong with it.
Harold: No, not until they filled it in. Filth. Filth. *(He opens the magazine at the crossword puzzle)* Right the way through from one across to thirty-eight down. A chequered square of concentrated filth, obscenity and hard core pornography.
Albert: It's not that bad. No worse than my Scrabble games.
Harold: Not that bad? There's three old ladies been treated for shock down the Darby and Joan Club.
Albert: If they didn't know the words they couldn't have filled it in, could they?
Harold: No, but I know somebody who will be filled in.
Albert: I don't know what you're going on about. The vicar didn't say anything.

Harold: 'Course he didn't. Poor old devil. He didn't understand the clues let alone the answers. Thank you very much again. That's seven nights' hard graft on my part at this moment coming out in smoke from the incinerator down the local nick.

Albert: You've got a copy of your article – what's the matter with you?

Harold: Yes, I have. And may I add that this, along with the few other copies that eluded the police dragnet, are now changing hands at twice the price of the School Kids edition of *Oz*. I am now going up to my room. (*He goes to the door. He turns*) I have just three things to say to you.

Albert: What's that?

Harold: Six across, thirteen across and twenty-eight down.

Albert: (*thinks quickly then explodes*) Don't you use language like that to me!

(*Harold goes out of the room. Albert follows him*)

Harold: Up your 14 across.

Albert: I will not be spoken to like that, do you hear? I'm your father.

Harold: Not according to 16 down.

Albert: You filthy, loud-mouthed swine.

Harold: Get 19'd across.

(*They exit upstairs*)

A Star Is Born

First transmission 28 February 1972

***A Star Is Born* featured**
Trevor Bannister as Rupert
with Margaret Nolan as Nemone
and was produced by John Howard Davies

SCENE 1

The Steptoes' yard. It is afternoon. The cart is standing there with a poster on its side advertising the amateur drama festival. Harold is sorting through a pile of junk. He has a sheet of paper in his hand. He picks out an old Victorian oil lamp.

Harold: That'll do. (*He puts it in a big cardboard box and ticks off his list*) One Victorian oil lamp. Four swords – we've got them inside. (*Ticks off his list*) Assorted cane furniture (*He sorts through the junk and finds a broken-down cane armchair*) Clean that up, that'll be all right. We've got some more of them somewhere. (*Ticks off his list*) Indian carpet – in my bedroom. (*Ticks off his list*) One stuffed tiger – that's going to be difficult.

    (*Albert comes into the yard carrying a shopping bag. He goes up to Harold who has his back to him*)

Harold: Oh gorblimey, curry again.

Albert: How do you know?

Harold: I could smell you coming down the street.

Albert: You like curry.

Harold: I know I do, but we've had it five times this week. And it's still only Thursday. We had it once for breakfast. Look at me, I'm turning brown.

Albert: It does you good in this weather. Warms you up, mate. Look at that lot – nine and a tanner. I don't know how he does it.

Harold: I do, mate. When did you last see a cat round here?

Albert: Ugh. If you don't want any, I'll have it. I'll cook you something else.

Harold: No, thank you. I've had enough of your Jimmy Young cock-ups.

Albert: *(looking in cardboard box)* What are you doing with them?

Harold: If you must know, I'm getting some props together for the next production at the Civic Hall.

Albert: Oh gawd, are they on the ear'ole again?

Harold: It's good publicity. We get a credit in the programme: 'Costumes and properties by Steptoe & Son'. *(He enters hall)*

Albert: Urgh!! *(He enters hall)*

SCENE 2
The hall.

Albert: I don't know why you bother. People don't want to see that rubbish. That last one you dragged me along to – *Richard the Hundred and Eleventh—*

Harold: *Richard the Third.*

Albert: Yeah. Terrible.

Harold: Shakespeare, terrible?

Albert: It was the way they did it. Ten people in the audience, including us. What a disaster. The curtain goes up, matey hobbles on, 'Now is the winter of our discontent', and his hump falls off. They're amateurs, Harold.

Harold: Of course they're amateurs, that's why it is so worth while. As it happens they are developing into a very good little company. Very competent, and I for one am very proud to be associated with them.

Albert: Cobblers! All you're interested in is knocking off the leading lady.

Harold: That has got nothing to do with it. I admit I do admire Madelaine Bannerman very much, but purely on an artistic level.

Albert: What's all that stuff for, then? What load of old rubbish are they doing this week?

Harold: We are performing a new play that has been specially written for us by our producer, Rupert Faines-Muir, and we are performing it at the Civic Hall next week.

Albert: We?

Harold: Yes, **we**. I'm in it.

Albert: You? On the stage?

Harold: And why not?

Albert: *(killing himself laughing)* Oh no – don't – stop it, don't make me laugh. *(Holds himself)* Oh dear oh dear.

Harold: I fail to see anything amusing.

Albert: *(posh voice)* Hello darling. Oh hello, dwarling. Oh lovely, dwarling. Saw your Hamlet, dwarling. Up yours, dwarling. Kiss my backside, dwarling.

Harold: *(stone-faced)* It's not like that at all.

Albert: 'Course it is. Actors – they're all poufs. All that make-up, love it they do. Love it.

Harold: I don't think I care to continue this discussion. Pray excuse me. *(Harold goes into the lounge carrying the box. Albert follows him)*

SCENE 3
The lounge. Harold puts the box on the table and starts emptying it. Albert comes in.

Albert: What are you going to call yourself? Lawrence O'Toole? *(Harold reacts)* Don't be silly, Harold, you'll only make a fool of yourself. You can't act. It takes years to learn, you have to go to school.

    (Harold is sorting out some swords, gun belts and Sam Brownes from a trunk)

Harold: Not necessarily. Lots of actors have started in rep. It's the finest experience you can get. I mean, Richard the Third, he's never been to drama school. He's an income tax inspector. Rupert says I'm a natural. He was very impressed with my audition.

Albert: Oh yes, what did you give him? Hamlet, Shylock, Henry the Fifth . . .?

Harold: Well, no, it was all a bit sudden, they sort of sprung it on me. I didn't have time to learn anything. I was scene shifting at the time, and the leading man dropped out – he's been transferred to another bus garage – and I happened to be there and so I just got up and did it.

Albert: What?

Harold: Marlon Brando. The taxi scene from *On the Waterfront.* You know – *(imitates Brando)* 'Oh Charlie, Charlie, oh no, Charlie, Charlie, I'm your brother, Charlie, I could have been the champ, Charlie, I was world class, Charlie, I did it for you, Charlie, I took a dive for you, I – oh Charlie, Charlie.' Well, you know how it goes.

Albert: And they gave you the job?

Harold: Well, yeah.

Albert: Cor, stuff my old boots.

Harold: They thought I was very good. He said I've got potential. And he's been around. He's a professional. I've seen his press cuttings – Oldham, Bradford, Barnsley.

Albert: If he's such a good actor, why ain't he in the West End?

Harold: He had to give up acting. He was very ill. It left him with a weak bladder and he can't stay on the stage for long periods.

Albert: Gorblimey, a right Goon Show this is going to be.

Harold: Typical, ain't it? You don't give anybody any credit for trying. It would get right up your nose if I was to become a star, wouldn't it? You'd be choked up to here. You'd hate to see me get on, wouldn't you? You'd hate to see me get out of this rat hole and – and get to the top. Making films all over the world – Rome, Madrid, Hollywood – playing opposite all that international crumpet – Racquel Welch, Jane Fonda, Virna Lisa . . .

Albert: Ooh – Irene Handl, that's more your mark.

Harold: I would be very honoured to play opposite Miss Handl. Because, don't you make any mistakes, it could happen. This could be what I've been waiting for. I've got a feeling. This is one job where an education don't matter. You don't need any A-levels to be an actor. For years I've been stuck here not knowing which way to go, not knowing how to express myself. I never thought about acting. This could be it. I'm not building castles in the air, Dad, I realize you have to have a bit of luck, but it happens to other people, why not me? I'm not a bad-looking feller. If Hollywood got hold of me, they'd do my nose and my teeth, and pin my ears back, I could look as good as any of them.

Albert: So could King Kong if they did that to him. Stop dreaming, Harold, it don't happen to blokes like you.

Harold: It does. Sean Connery was a lorry driver, he's the same age as me, and I've got more hair than he has. Oh, I didn't expect any help from you, but you'll be the first one to board my yacht, won't you? Well, I've got news for you, you're barred. The moment I see you walking up that gangplank, I shall tell the captain 'Full steam ahead, and see if you can get him with the propellers'.

Albert: Bah, the only yacht you'll ever see is that plastic one in your bath.

Harold: We shall see. And now, if you wouldn't mind serving dinner, I have a lot of work to do. At eight o'clock the entire company are meeting here . . .

Albert: Eh?

Harold: For our first rehearsal. A new play by Rupert Faines-Muir, a drama of the North-West Frontier entitled . . .

Albert: *Up your Khyber.*

Harold: Entitled *Guilt. The White Man's Burden.* And introducing . . . *(he takes out a uniform from the trunk and holds it up against himself)* . . . Harold Steptoe as Lieutenant Carstairs, VC and Bar, of the 1st Battalion Royal Indian Rifles.

Albert: In a Polish cavalry uniform?

Harold: It can be dyed and altered, they won't notice the difference.

Albert: They will round here, mate, there'll be more turbans in the audience than on stage. What are they rehearsing round here for?

Harold: Because the Karate Club are using the hall tonight. Now hurry up.

(Albert has opened the tin foil containers with food in. He gives Harold a spoon and they eat straight from the containers)

Albert: Here you are, chicken Madras and mutton vindaloo. Get that down you, it might help you to get into character.

(Harold sits down and puts some curry into his mouth. It is very hot. He grasps his throat, rushes to the sideboard and squirts a soda siphon into his mouth)

Harold: *(croaking)* Oh gawd, my voice, my voice. If I make my debut sounding like Louis Armstrong I'll murder you.

SCENE 4

The lounge. It is evening. A semi-circle of chairs has been placed in the centre of the room. Albert is finishing his dinner.

Harold enters dressed in a double-breasted blazer, grey flannels, cravat and dark glasses, with a pipe in his mouth.

Albert: Hallo, have you bought your yacht already?

Harold: Haven't you gone out yet? They'll be here in a minute. Here's ten bob, go to the pictures.

Albert: I've seen it.

Harold: Go and see it again.

Albert: I don't want to.

(The door bell rings)

Harold: Oh gawd, they're here. Dad, please go out, I don't ask you for much.

Albert: No. It's too cold.

Harold: Go to bed then.

Albert: No. It's too early.

Harold: Right. Stay here. But I'm warning you ... *(he takes a scimitar)* ... this is very important to me. One word out of place from you, and the next item on the menu will be curried goolies, all right? *(The door bell rings again)* Watch it, that's all.

Albert: Yes, dwarling. Anything you say, dwarling.

(Harold reacts)

SCENE 5

The hall. Harold and Albert go out into the hall. Harold opens the door.

Harold: Oh, you found it all right. Do come in.

(Five people come in, four men and a woman)

Rupert: Come on, darlings, in you go.

Woman: Hello, darling. *(Kisses Harold)*

Harold: Hello.

Woman: *(to one of the men)* Be a darling, darling, take my .coat, darling.

Man: Yes, darling!

Woman: Thank you, darling.

(He takes her coat. Albert reacts with a sneer; Harold realizes what he means and looks away)

Rupert: *(to someone still outside)* Do come in, darling, get the door closed. *(Another girl comes in – a beautiful, voluptuous girl)* Now, I don't believe you know everybody. This is our new leading lady, Nemone Wagstaffe. *(He introduces the girl. Harold is open mouthed)*

Harold: How do you do.

(They shake hands, she holds on to his)

Nemone: Hello. I've heard so much about you.

Harold: Have you? All good, I hope. *(Chuckles nervously)* Um . . . er, what happened to Miss Bannerman?

Rupert: Yes, what indeed. *(The others giggle)* No, do let me tell this one. You know she was married, don't you?

Harold: No I didn't.

Rupert: Oh yes, she was married to Norman who worked the lights. It was a bit umpty, we were all expecting something. Anyway, you remember Jack, who played Jim in *John Loves Jane*?

Harold: Oh yes.

Rupert: Well, he was married to Janice who played his mother . . . well, it seems that Jack came home from work last night, packed his bags and went. There's an empty desk at the Gas Board showrooms this morning.

Harold: Went? Just like that?

Rupert: Scarpered, with the Bannerman. They've gone into production on their own. We're very lucky to have got hold of Nemone . . . tremendous experience.

Harold: Really?

Rupert: A right little pro, aren't you, darling?

Nemone: (*straight to Harold*) I shall look forward to playing opposite you . . . Harold.

Harold: Oh . . . I hope I won't let you down. I'm very inexperienced.

Nemone: I'm sure not in everything.

Harold: (swallows) Won't you all come into the lounge?

SCENE 6
They all file into the room, Rupert looks around.

Rupert: Oh I say, what about this? What a super set. Straight out of *Love on the Dole*.

Albert: This is our home.

Rupert: Oh, I didn't mean to be rude.

Harold: (*jumping in*) May I introduce my father – Father, this is our producer, Rupert Faines-Muir.

Albert: How do you do.

Rupert: Delighted.

Albert: I'm sorry to hear about your illness. If you get caught short, the bog's outside.

Harold: Er . . . anyone like a drink?

Rupert: Nothing alcoholic, we've got work to do.

Harold: Would you like some cocoa?

Rupert: Yes, yes, cocoa will be fine.

Harold: (*to Albert*) Go and make some cocoa.

Albert: No, I want to watch.

Harold: Go and make some cocoa. (*He takes hold of the scimitar again and raises it from the ground in between Albert's legs. Albert rises with it*) With milk. (*Albert delicately lifts his leg over the scimitar and goes out*) I'm terribly sorry for the delay.

Rupert: Yes, well, come along. Let's get started. You've all got your words.

(*They sit down, some on the chairs, one of the girls on the floor. They flick through the scripts they are holding*)

Harold: I've got most of the props together, I think you'll be pleased with them. I've got some uniforms as well. (*He points to the uniforms*)

Rupert: Oh yes, lovely.

Harold: And I must say I've read the play and I think it's quite magnificent.

Rupert: Thank you, dear boy.

Harold: I only hope your confidence in me is not misplaced and I don't make a co – a ball – I don't mess it up.

Rupert: My dear boy, I've never been wrong yet. In any case I love the challenge of presenting a new face to my public. Now, briefly, the play takes place in a beleaguered fort on the Indian frontier during the Afghan rising. A punitive expedition by the British has failed and they are now surrounded by fifty thousand savage tribesmen – whom we don't see, of course. The dramatis personae . . .

Harold: The what?

Rupert: The cast . . . are the Officer Commanding the Fort, General Sir Langham Willoughby – that's you Jeremy – and his wife Lady Cecilia – Deirdre – their beautiful daughter Ariadne – Nemone, and her fiancé Lieutenant Carstairs – that's you, Harold (*Harold pulls his shoulders back proudly*) Also in the Fort are Gunga Din – Manville, blacking up again, I'm afraid – and the General's batman – you, Timmy.

Deirdre: Rupert, darling, I don't wish to knock it at this stage but don't you think the plot is just an incey-wincey bit, well . . . old fashioned . . . for 1972, I mean?

Rupert: I thought you'd read it, darling.

Deirdre: I have, darling.

Rupert: Then surely you must have realized that is deliberate. The whole thing is an analogy between the British in India and the Americans in Vietnam.

(*The cast exchange looks and mutter in surprise, evidently not having realized that*)

Harold: Well, that's the first thing that struck me, that's why I liked it so much. It has a profound social message, I think . . . for us all.

Rupert: *(beaming)* Thank you, Harold. Thank God for an intelligent actor.

Harold: *(modestly)* It's probably that I've had more time to study it than my fellow players.

Rupert: The only other member of the cast is a special government envoy, the Right Honourable the Lord Carruthers, KC, who has been personally sent by Queen Victoria to negotiate with the Mad Mullah. Unfortunately we've got a bit of a problem there.

Harold: Why's that.

Rupert: Reg hasn't turned up. He had all his teeth out this morning and he won't get his new set made till after we open. It's going to be a difficult part to cast. Lord Carruthers is a man of seventy, a distinguished career behind him. Military bearing, a patrician-like face, small stature, but—

(The door opens and Albert comes in carrying a tray loaded with mugs, tin cups and cups and saucers, none of which matches)

Albert: Come and get it. *(He puts the tray down on the table. Rupert is staring at him)*

Rupert: Don't move.

Albert: Eh?

Rupert: Say that again.

Albert: Say what again?

Rupert: What you just said.

Albert: Come and get it.

Rupert: Remarkable. Such resonance. *(He gets up and walks round Albert looking him up and down. He places his hand under Albert's chin and turns his profile round)* Amazing. Walk over to the door. *(Albert walks to the door)* Turn around. *(Albert turns a circle)* Now back. *(Albert walks back)* It's incredible.

Harold: No.

Rupert: Pardon?

Harold: I'm not having him in it.

Rupert: But he's perfect. Look at that face. That is the Right Honourable the Lord Carruthers to a tee.

Harold: That is my dad who is an ignorant old git. And if he's in it, he'll ruin it.

Rupert: I don't think so. *(To Albert)* Have you ever been on the stage before?

Harold: No.

Albert: Yes.

Harold: When?

Albert: The '14-'18 War. Troop concerts.

Harold: Oh, of course, you've done everything, haven't you? If we needed a brain surgeon, you'd be first up, wouldn't you? Give the cocoa round. Rupert, can I have a word with you in private?

Rupert: Certainly.

(They walk to the other side of the room. As they pass Albert, he is handing a tin mug to Nemone. Harold takes the mug and hands her a cup and saucer. He takes the saucer and changes it for a matching one. He smiles at her, then snarls at the old man)

Harold: Why don't you sod off? *(He joins Rupert on the other side of the room)* Rupert, you're making a big mistake. He can't play a lord with a voice like that.

Rupert: He talks like you.

Harold: But I'm like Michael Caine. I can put it on, like he did in *Zulu.*

Rupert: Perhaps your father can.

Harold: He can't. He's as coarse as cowcakes.

Rupert: *(calls to Albert)* Mr Steptoe, can you speak in an upper-class accent?

Albert: *(posh voice)* What, you mean like this, old chap?

Rupert: See, he's perfect.

Harold: He's not perfect. He's rotten.

Albert: *(posh voice)* Of course, if you want him more Sandhurst there was an officer in my regiment who had a frightfully interesting voice . . . more like . . .

Harold: Shut up! He'll never keep it up. He's right gorblimey.

Rupert: I think we'll take a chance on him. Mr Steptoe, how would you like to play Lord Carruthers?

Albert: Yeah, I'll give it a go. It might be a giggle.

(Harold reacts)

Rupert: The part is marked.

Harold: All right, I've warned you, he'll be a disaster. Be it on your own heads. *(He sits)*

Rupert: Right, we'll go from the top. The scene opens at dusk. There is a lull in the fighting. All is quiet. The curtain rises and we find Lieutenant Carstairs on the veranda with Ariadne in his arms. Over here.

(Harold and Nemone, with their scripts open, go to the middle of the

room. Rupert poses them, Harold with his arm round Nemone. She squeezes up to him. Harold tries not to look down the front of her dress)

Rupert: Right. Go.

Nemone: It's very quiet out there.

Harold: Yes.

Nemone: It's unbelievably quiet.

Harold: Yes.

Nemone: Do you think they will attack before morning?

Harold: No.

Nemone: You're very taciturn, aren't you?

Harold: Yes.

Albert: Blimey, you've got a bit part, haven't you?

Rupert: Ssh, ssh, ssh.

Harold: I told you he's not a professional, he won't take it seriously.

Rupert: Now come along, no temperament. Carry on. Keep it going.

Nemone: What chance do you think we have, darling?

Harold: There's one chance in a million. If we slip out of here tonight, and if I get to Delhi in the morning . . .

Albert: *(sings quietly)* Ding, dong, the bells are going to chime . . .

Harold: *(throws his script down)* I'll kill him, I'll kill him, get him out of here.

Rupert: *(to Albert)* Mr Steptoe, you're not giving your son a chance. Come along, let's be serious. Carry on, Harold, you're very good. Your speech, Nemone.

Nemone: Do you think we'll get out of this alive?

Harold: He won't if he don't turn it in.

Rupert: Stick to the script, please.

Harold: I'm sorry. Your father and Lord Carruthers are in the study now discussing the terms they will present to the Mad Mullah.

Nemone: Don't you mean the terms the Mad Mullah will present to us?

Harold: *(brave laugh)* I should have known it was foolish to try and deceive a soldier's daughter. But believe me, Ariadne, I promise you I won't let those fiends take you alive. I have saved the last two bullets for us. That way we shall always be . . . together.

Nemone: My darling.

(They kiss)

Rupert: The door bursts open and in stride Lord Carruthers and the General. Lord Carruthers is angry. Go.

Albert: I won't bother too much with the accent. I'll work on it later. (*Albert and the General open an imaginary door*) I am not satisfied, Willoughby, Her Majesty's Government has been seriously misled (*pronounced 'mizzled'*) (*Harold looks at the old man's script then at his own*)

Harold: That's mis-led.

Albert: Oh, sorry. Misled. But needless (*pronounced 'needles'*) to say . . .

Harold: Need-less. I told you, he's going to spoil it.

Rupert: That's all right, we'll sort it out. Go on, go on.

Albert: But needless to say I have a plan. I bring a sausage from Her Majesty . . .

Harold: Message! Put your bleeding glasses on. Can't you rewrite it? Can't you have him stand at the French windows and get killed by a stray bullet?

Rupert: No, no, don't stop, carry on.

Harold: What is the sausage – the message you bring?

Albert: It is a message from Her Majesty the Queen to Alf Garnett's chief.

Rupert: The Afghan chief.

Albert: Yes. The Afghan chief. It is a message of peace and goodwill between our two peoples and as a gesture of friendship she has instructed me to present to the Mad Mullah a string of poloponies.

Harold: Polop – polo ponies!

Albert: That's not my fault, it's the bleeding typist, she's run the words into each other.

Harold: It's the same in my script, I have to say it as well. I knew they were polo ponies. She wouldn't give him a string of poloponies, would she?

Albert: Well, I don't know what Afghans have for breakfast.

Harold: You can't read, you can't think and you can't act, and the whole production is going to be a fiasco.

Rupert: Now, now darling. It's early days. It's just a read-through.

Harold: And my career is going to be in ruins before it's even started. (*He has stalked to the door, he opens it, he turns back*) Poloponies. You great berk. (*He goes out and slams the door. They all look at the door in consternation*)

SCENE 7

The stage of the Civic Hall. It is the night of the performance. The entire company are lined up in their costumes, holding hands, taking their bows to enthusiastic applause. They are lined up in the following order: Gunga Din, General's wife, Nemone, Harold, General, the Mad Mullah, Albert. Gunga Din and the Mad Mullah step forward for their individual bow. Polite applause. The General and his wife step forward. Polite applause. Nemone steps forward. Polite applause. Albert steps forward. Tumultuous applause and cheering. Harold steps forward. Less applause than anybody. They all look to Albert at the end of the line. They put their arms out to him. He reacts with a 'What, me?' expression and steps forward. More tumultuous applause and cheering. He walks along and stands in front of the line, graciously acknowledging the applause. The cast also applaud him, except Harold, who has a sour, frozen, clenched-teeth smile on his face.

SCENE 8

Harold's dressing room at the Civic Hall. Harold is on his own, and miserable. A crate of beer, bottles of Scotch and sherry and glasses are on the table. He has almost finished dressing. From next door there is the sound of a party in progress.

The door opens and a young man comes in.

Young Man: Good evening, I'm the drama critic of the *East Acton Gazette.*

Harold: *(lights up)* Oh . . . please come in. Have a drink?

Young Man: No, thank you, I've got one next door. Your father sent me in to ask you if you were going to join him in the celebrations.

Harold: Er, no, if he'll excuse me, I've got a bit of a headache. It's a very demanding part, I feel quite exhausted.

Young Man: Yes, yes, of course. I'll be off, then. Enjoyed it very much. By the way, as a matter of interest, something you said in the third act confused me . . . what is a polopony?

Harold: Oh, it was just a slip of the tongue. I made a mistake, that was all.

Young Man: I see. Cheers.

(He goes out. Harold puts on his coat. He puts the bottle of Scotch in his pocket, has a look round the dressing room. He puts the light out and goes out into the corridor. He stops outside Albert's open dressing room

door. It is packed with people all drinking and chatting gaily. Albert is the centre of attraction. He is being very grand and animated as he chats to everybody. Harold walks on down the corridor.

SCENE 9
The empty stage. The scenery has been flown. Harold wanders on to the stage. He walks to the centre of the stage and looks out into the hall. There is the sound of a Covent Garden-type ovation. He bows. Cut to a stock shot of an evening-dressed audience at a large theatre, all on their feet applauding, cheering. Cut back to Harold standing alone on the empty stage. The audience soundtrack fades away.

Harold turns and walks slowly to the back of the stage to the exit door. He opens it and goes out into the street. He passes Albert's frosted-glass dressing-room window. It is lit. There is the sound of the party inside. Harold stops for a moment, then walks on a few yards. A little boy comes up to him with an autograph book.

Little Boy: Here, mister, are you an actor?
Harold: No, son. I'm a rag and bone man.
    (The little boy goes away. Harold looks at the dressing-room window. He takes out his bottle of Scotch and hurls it through the window. He turns and runs off down the street as fast as he can)

SCENE 10
The lounge. Harold walks in, crosses to the bar, picks up a glass, crosses to the table – and realizes he has thrown his whisky away.

Oh, What A Beautiful Mourning

First transmission 6 March 1972

Oh, What A Beautiful Mourning featured
George A. Cooper as Uncle Arthur
with
Mollie Sugden
Rita Webb
Yvonne Antrobus
Bartlett Mullins
Tommy Godfrey
Queenie Watts
Stella Moray
Margaret Flint
Simon Cord
Gilly Flower
and was produced by John Howard Davies

SCENE 1
Harold drives the horse and cart into the forecourt of a petrol station. He drives on to the empty side of the pumps. On the other side is a motorist filling up his radiator from a hosepipe.
   An attendant pumps up the tyres of the cart from the air pump. Harold takes the hosepipe, fills up a bucket and waters the horse.

SCENE 2
The hall of the Steptoes' house. Albert picks up the mail, sorts through it, comes to a black-edged envelope. He reacts. He opens it, and takes out a black-edged card. He reads it and reacts with sorrow.

SCENE 3

Back at the petrol station, the horse and cart is now in a line of cars queuing up for the automatic car wash. The horse and cart go in. A few minutes later the horse and cart are standing at the other end of the car wash having gone through it. Harold is wiping the horse down. The cart is dripping wet. An attendant comes up to Harold. Harold pays him. The attendant gives him two Green Shield stamps. Harold nods to a sign that reads 'Quadruple Green Shield Stamps'. The attendant gives him some more. Harold gets on the cart and drives off.

SCENE 4

The Steptoes' lounge. Albert is sitting at the table with the black-edged card in his hand. He is gazing into the distance. Harold enters.

Harold: Here you are, another eight Green Shield Stamps. (*He offers them to the old man. Albert ignores him*) Here you are, don't you want them? Another half a million and you can get that motor-bike you always wanted. (*Albert just stares into the distance*) Are you all right, Dad?

Albert: Your Uncle George is dead.

Harold: Oh gawd, not another bleeding funeral.

Albert: That's a nice thing to say.

Harold: Well, we've had a bellyful, haven't we? Six in the last two years. Your brothers and sisters are dropping like flies.

Albert: Well, there are fourteen of us. It's the law of averages. Some of them are bound to go.

Harold: Yeah. How are *you* feeling?

Albert: Don't you worry about me, mate. I'll get my telegram from the Queen, don't you bother.

Harold: Only to ask when you're going. Oh, I hate them Steptoe funerals. It don't seem to matter how many of them go, there's always the same number there. They drop like flies and breed like rabbits.

Albert: We're a very close-knit family.

Harold: Get out of it! That's the only time they see each other, at funerals. Five hours of sheer naked hatred and avarice. (*Mimics two old women*) 'He said I could have his watch.' 'No, he didn't, he gave it to me.' 'Who was it looked after him?' 'Only when you knew he was going.' I'm not going through all that again. It's obscene.

Albert: *(rising)* I don't care, we are going and that's the end of it.

Harold: *(fed up)* When is it?

Albert: Friday. *(He sits)*

Harold: Oh, that's marvellous. That's my yoga night gone for the chop. Same place, I suppose.

Albert: Of course. The Steptoes have been buried there since 1842.

Harold: Yeah, I know. You could build a council estate on the ground they take up. Which one was Uncle George, anyway?

Albert: My eldest brother.

Harold: I can't remember him – there's so many of them.

Albert: You wouldn't remember him, you haven't seen him since you was six months old.

Harold: Why?

Albert: He was your godfather.

Harold: I thought godfathers were supposed to look after your religious upbringing and buy you presents on your birthday and stuff.

Albert: That's right, that's why you never saw him. We made a mistake choosing him. Tight as a gnat's chuff, he was. He was the only man I know who used to bring his hair home from the barber's.

Harold: Get away.

Albert: Yeah. He used to stuff his cushions with it.

Harold: I should think he must be worth a few bob, then?

Albert: Oh, yes. He hasn't left the house for thirty years, never went anywhere, never spent anything. Yes, it'll be a big turn-out, this one. They'll all be there.

Harold: Let's give it a miss Dad. You don't really want to go, do you? They don't like you, and you don't like them, you've always said that.

Albert: Exactly. That's why I like going. I shall see them all off one after the other. It's the only enjoyment I get these days. Besides, I want to be there for the share-out. If there's anything going, I'm having it.

Harold: Gorblimey, you're as bad as the rest of them.

Albert: He borrowed twenty-five quid off me in 1927 'to emigrate to Australia to start a new life', he said. The nearest he got to Sydney was the Dog and Duck, Wood Green. And I never got my money back. As far as I'm concerned, I'm entitled to first pickings on whatever he's left. And if I'm not there I've had it. 'Cos the minute they've put him away, they'll be through that house like a plague of locusts. There'll be nothing left. It'll be picked clean. It'll be down to the floorboards. You won't realize anybody ever lived there.

Harold: Oh, isn't it touching? It gets you right there. *(taps his chest)* What a family. They make the bleeding Borgias look like the Archers. I wouldn't mind if they were honest about it, but I can't stand the hypocrisy. 'Hallo Ted, hallo Minnie, hallo Jessie, a sad occasion, he was a lovely feller. Salt of the earth. One of the best. He'll be sadly missed.' They'll all be standing round the hole crying their eyes out.

Albert: 'Course they will, that's half the fun. You can't have a funeral without a few tears, it's not right.

Harold: I suppose Potty Aida will be there again. Lifting her skirts up in front of the vicar.

Albert: Well, she's harmless. And after all she is your auntie.

Harold: I don't know, there's some dodgy strains in that family. Well, I'm not looking after her, I got lumbered with her last time. In the same car. She was effing and blinding all the way down the Goldhawk Road. I mean, she must be knocking on sixty and she still dresses like Carmen Miranda.

Albert: It's not her fault, Harold. She went a bit funny in 1940. Her world ended when Sid never came back from Dunkirk.

Harold: He came back all right, he just never went home. He's up in Newcastle. We all know that – why doesn't somebody tell her? Poor cow.

Albert: Don't be cruel, Harold. She's better off as she is.

Harold: And I suppose Uncle Nobby will be there – the Malcolm Muggeridge of the family. I suppose he'll get me in the corner again, give me an hour's lecture on the meaning of life and death, how we've all got to look for God, tap me for a fiver and straight round the boozer before Alice sees him.

Albert: I won't hear anything against young Nobby. He's the only one I've got any time for. He's got a lot to put up with, with Alice. I mean, how would you like to find out none of your five kids are yours? It was natural he turned to God. He's very religious when he's sober. He was one of Billy Graham's first converts, he was, at the Albert Hall. He went up on stage, and he told the whole audience his problems. And Billy Graham turned to him, and said 'Take courage, my son, take courage.'

Harold: Yeah, and he's been bleeding drinking it ever since. Well, I'm telling you, Dad, if you insist on me going . . .

Albert: You got to go, all your cousins will be there.

Harold: All right. But I'm not wearing that black suit again. I shall wear an armband.

Albert: You'll wear the black suit. You're not showing me up in front of my family.

Harold: I've worn it the last sixteen times. It's out of date.

Albert: We're going to a funeral not a fashion parade.

Harold: Dad, it's got turn-ups.

Albert: Then cut the bloody things off. You're wearing a black suit, a black tie, black shoes, a white shirt and bowler hat.

Harold: I'm not wearing a bowler hat.

SCENE 5
The hall. Harold enters wearing a black suit, a black tie, black shoes, a white shirt and a bowler hat.

Harold: *(calling up the stairs)* Dad, are you ready? Hurry up, kick-off's in half an hour. There'll be another three gone by the time we get there.

(Albert comes downstairs. He is also in a black suit and bowler hat)

Albert: Right, I'm ready. Come on.

Harold: Oh, this is ridiculous. Can't we go out separately? We look like a couple of pox doctor's clerks. Well, come on, let's get it over with.

Albert: Have you sent the wreath?

Harold: No. I thought we'd nick one off one of the other graves on the way in.

Albert: We can't do that. I told you—

Harold: Of course I've sent the wreath.

Albert: Did you put a message on it?

Harold: What do you want a message on it for, he can't read it. He's dead.

Albert: It's not for him, it's for the others. Now nobody'll know who sent it. I knew I should have done it myself, wasting all that money.

Harold: Hurry up, the car's outside.

Albert: Have they sent a car? I thought the cars went from the house of the deceased.

Harold: I'm not going on a bus dressed like this. I've hired a car to take us.

Albert: What did you get?

Harold: A mustard yellow drop-head with wire wheels.

Albert: Harold, you haven't! We can't go to a funeral in a racing car.

Harold: It's not going that's important, it's the coming back. You want to be first back from the cemetery for the share-out, don't you? *They* won't be hanging about, mate. As soon as the vicar closes the book it'll be a massed racing start back to the house. Half a dozen limousines haring over the flyover. It'll be like one of those land-grabs on the cowboy films. What a degrading spectacle this is going to be. Come on, let's get going.

Albert: I'm not going in a yellow sports car.

Harold: Oh, don't be daft. I've got a black saloon. You've got no sense of humour, have you? Now come on. (*They go to the door, Albert takes out a handkerchief, sniffs and dabs his eyes*) Now what are you doing?

Albert: I'm crying.

Harold: What for?

Albert: There might be some neighbours looking.

Harold: (*shoving him out of the door*) Get out there.

SCENE 6

The front room of Uncle George's house. In the middle of the room is a coffin standing on trestles, wreaths and flowers all round it. There are glasses and bottles of beer on the coffin lid. The Steptoe family, all in full mourning, are gathered in the room. One of the men picks up a glass from the coffin, takes a swig and puts it back. A group of men are standing listening to Uncle Arthur telling a joke. The women of the family and the rest of the men are walking round the room, examining and appraising the furniture, ornaments, pictures, etc, picking them up, turning them upside down, making notes on their lists, just like an auction room.

Harold and Albert enter. They take off their bowlers. They watch the family examining the contents. They put their bowlers on a side table. No one has noticed their arrival.

Albert: Hallo, they're at it already. I'm surprised they haven't had a catalogue printed.

(*An old man standing nearby is examining a vase. He puts it down, makes a mark on his list and then picks up Albert's bowler and examines it. He feels the lining, taps the crown. Albert snatches it from him and puts it back on his head)*

Albert: Oi, that's mine.

Old man: *(squinting at Albert)* Oh hallo, Albert. I thought it was George's.

Harold: I shouldn't think he's got anything left, has he?

Old man: Oh no, we're still sticking to the rules. Nothing goes till *he's* gone.

(Uncle Nobby is sitting on his own in the corner with a Bible in one hand and an empty glass in the other, dead drunk)

Nobby: The wages of sin are death, we are all doomed.

Harold: Oh gawd, Uncle Nobby's at it again.

Nobby: Armageddon is upon us.

Auntie Minnie: Oh, gawd, turn it in, Nobby. Fill his glass, somebody.

(One of the men fills his glass up with Scotch)

Nobby: Cheers, your very good health.

(Arthur finishes telling his joke. The group listening to him all laugh. Arthur then spots Albert and Harold standing on their own, and his face immediately freezes to a mournful expression. He goes over to them)

Arthur: Hallo, Albert.

Albert: Hallo, Arthur.

Arthur: A very sad occasion for us all.

Albert: Yeah. I expect we'll get over it. You know Harold.

Arthur: Yes of course. Hallo, Harold.

Harold: Hallo, Uncle Arthur.

Arthur: The last time we met was at Freda's interment . . . or was it Bob's?

Harold: I can't remember, I lose track. Auntie Freda was the last one.

Arthur: Yes, that's right. Freda. *(Fingers his tiepin)* Bob was the tiepin. Well, I expect you could do with a drink like us all – help us get through the day.

Albert: I'll have a brown ale.

Harold: Scotch and ginger.

Arthur: *(calls)* Elsie, dear. Brown ale and Scotch and ginger.

Albert: You're in charge again, are you, Arthur?

Arthur: The family asked me to look after the arrangements.

Harold: Well, you've had enough practice, haven't you?

Arthur: Yes, yes, sadly.

Harold: You ought to be training somebody else up. I mean who's going to look after you when you go?

Arthur: *(chuckling sourly)* Let's hope that won't be too soon.

(Elsie comes over with a quart bottle of brown and a glass and a tumbler of Scotch. She gives Harold the Scotch and puts the quart of brown and the beer glass on the coffin)

Elsie: Here you are, Uncle Albert. Help yourself. The sausage rolls are over there.

Albert: Well, this is a very significant occasion today.

Arthur: Oh, why's that, then?

Albert: That's the first bleeding drink I've had on him. Cheers.

Arthur: Good health.

(They drink)

Albert: How's things down the bus garage?

Arthur: Mustn't grumble.

Albert: Did he leave a will?

Harold: Oh gawd.

Arthur: Yes, he did. We'll be reading that when we come back.

Harold: I suppose you'll be reading it. Being the *executor*.

Arthur: *(smiles coldly)* Executor, Harold.

Harold: Of course, I'm so sorry.

Albert: Is it worth hanging about for?

Arthur: I'm sure we'll all be pleasantly surprised. He was quite comfortably off, you know, was George.

Albert: He was entitled to be, he never spent anything. Did he mention the twenty-five quid he nicked off me in 1927?

Arthur: I've no idea. I haven't read it. The solicitor handed it to me this morning. I am not at liberty to open it until after the interment.

(The old man walks up to them)

Old man: You've done him proud, Arthur.

Arthur: Thank you, Ted.

Old man: Yes, it's going to be a very nice send-off.

Arthur: Yes, the Co-op do a very good job.

Albert: Who's getting the divvy on it?

Arthur: That's a very tasteless remark, Albert.

Albert: Oh, it is you, then?

Arthur: I've had a great deal of personal expense, I'm entitled to the divvy. The insurance policy didn't cover the entire cost of the interment, you know.

Albert: He was ninety-three – how long do you have to pay into it?

Arthur: Albert, the cost of dying has risen quite considerably since

George took that policy out. I have a detailed list of my expenses and you will find that I personally am two pounds forty-five pence out of pocket.

Harold: Well, you can't expect to make a profit on all of them. You did very well out of Auntie Freda's.

Arthur: I beg your pardon, how dare you?

Harold: Come off it, we had a whip round for the flowers, we give you a pound each, and where did you get them from? Out of your garden.

Arthur: I let you have them cheaper than you would have got them in the shops.

Harold: I should think so. They were on their last legs.

Arthur: My blooms are the best in Acton. I go to a great deal of trouble rearing them. I win prizes every year.

Harold: They were on their last legs. It was a toss up who was deader, them or Auntie Freda. It was disgraceful. Going down Minerva Road a light breeze sprang up, there wasn't a petal left on them when we got to the cemetery.

Albert: Yeah, embarrassing it was. Poor old Freda, lying there under a great pile of stalks.

Arthur: The rest of the family are quite happy with my organization.

Albert: Well, I'm not.

Arthur: Am I to take it, Albert, that you won't be wanting me to arrange your funeral?

Harold: What? I wouldn't let you anywhere near his funeral. I'll take care of him. I know exactly what I'm going to do with him. I've had it worked out for years.

Albert: Harold . . .

Harold: When he goes, mate, he's going in style. It'll be the best funeral this family's ever seen. I'm only sorry he won't be here to see it.

Albert: Harold, don't keep talking about my funeral, you know it upsets me.

Harold: I'm sorry, Dad, I just wanted you to know that I won't let any of this lot get their grasping little hands on you. Look at them, it's like feeding time in the vulture house.

(The family are examining all the effects. Across the room two of the women start squabbling over a vase. They try to snatch it from each other)

Joyce: You can take your eyes off that. He promised that to me years ago.

Jessie: Oh no he didn't, he said I could have it.

Albert: Oh gawd, those two are off again.

Joyce: Who looked after him?

Jessie: Only when you knew he was going.

Joyce: You're not having it, you're not even family.

Jessie: I beg your pardon, I've been in this family for twenty-five years.

Joyce: You only started coming round here in the last couple of months though, didn't you?

Arthur: Excuse me. *(He goes over to the two women)* Now come along, girls, stop squabbling. There's enough for all of us.

Albert: *(to Harold)* Have you had a look round? Seen anything you fancy?

Elsie: Me, for instance?

Harold: Forget it, Dad, you don't stand a chance here. These are professional tomb robbers.

Albert: *(out of the corner of his mouth)* How much do you reckon on the two oil paintings?

Harold: Flumpence.

Albert: What about the Persian rug?

Harold: Belgian cotton. If you're really interested, the best thing here is the porcelain figurine on the mantelpiece. That is a very lovely piece. Limoges, eighteenth century.

Albert: Put your bowler hat over it.

(A young man approaches them)

Albert: Sshh, say nothing, the opposition.

Young man: Hello, Harold, isn't it?

Harold: That's right . . . um . . . er . . . *(trying to think of his name)*

Young man: Jeffrey – Arthur's son.

Harold: Of course.

Young man: Sad occasion, isn't it?

Harold: Oh yeah, heart-breaking.

Young man: Hello, Uncle Albert.

Albert: Hello.

Young man: Have you had a shufti round yet?

Albert: Er . . . no, no I haven't.

Young man: The best thing here is the porcelain group on the mantelpiece.

Albert: What, that? No – rubbish. I wouldn't give it house room. Reproduction. Woolies – I wouldn't waste your time with it.

Young man: That's eighteenth century.

Albert: Look, I know what I'm talking about, son, I'm in the business.

Young man: So am I, I've got a stall in the Portobello Road.

Harold: You were window cleaning last time I heard.

Young man: Yeah, well, there's no gelt in that, is there? *(Walks off)* Yes, Limoges that is, second quarter, eighteenth century.

Albert: See? I told you to put your bowler hat over it. He'll have that away now.

Harold: That's that Arthur Negus and his programme. The whole bleeding country are experts now. I'm going to get a drink.

(Harold walks across the room to the drink table. On his way he acknowledges some of the family, shakes a few hands, gets kissed by a couple of the old ladies.

An old lady walks up to Albert. This is his sister Minnie)

Minnie: Hello, Albert.

Albert: Hello, Minnie.

Minnie: He didn't suffer, you know.

Albert: Didn't he?

Minnie: No. Went out like a light. Went as he wanted to – with his boots on.

Albert: I bet he ain't got them now.

Minnie: Well, he was ninety-three, so he can't complain, can he? I suppose you'll be the next one, Albert?

Albert: Now that's not funny, Minnie. I got years to go yet.

Minnie: Got your eyes on anything?

Albert: Mind your own business.

Minnie: The only thing here worth having is the porcelain group on the mantelpiece. *(She wanders off. Albert scowls)*

(Harold is at the drink table. A young girl in full mourning comes up to him. This is his cousin Caroline. He smiles tentatively at her)

Caroline: You don't recognize me, do you, Harold?

Harold: You do have the advantage of me.

Caroline: I've been in your bed many times.

Harold: I beg your pardon?

Caroline: My mum used to leave me round your house when she worked at the dog track.

Harold: You're not little Caroline . . .?

Caroline: That's right. Alice's youngest.

Harold: That was twenty years ago. You were only about three. I bet she wouldn't leave you round there now.

Caroline: Now, now, Uncle Harold.

Harold: I'm not your uncle, I'm your cousin.

Caroline: *(archly)* Oh well, that's all right, then, isn't it?

Harold: Um . . . what are you doing after the funeral?

Caroline: I've got a little rave-up at a friend's pad tonight . . . interested?

Harold: *(looks round the room)* Is your mother here?

Caroline: She's upstairs going through the linen cupboard.

Harold: It is all right, isn't it – cousins?

Caroline: Oh yeah, no bother. We're well removed . . . at the moment. Can you pick me up?

Harold: Yeah. What time?

Caroline: Well, I've got to bring Mum back here for the share-out. Mind you, that won't take long. As far as I'm concerned, the only thing worth having is . . .

Both: The porcelain group on the mantelpiece.

Harold: Yeah, I know.

Caroline: Let's say six o'clock.

Harold: Right.

Caroline: See you later.

> *(She wanders off. Harold watches her with a smile. Albert sidles up to him)*

Albert: You want to keep away from that.

Harold: Why, what's it got to do with you?

Albert: She's Alice's girl.

Harold: Well, so what? Cousins is all right.

Albert: Yeah, but none of them are Nobby's. I told you that.

Harold: Well, that makes it even better then, don't it?

Albert: Well, we don't know, it could be any of us.

Harold: Oh gawd, what a bleeding family.

> *(Arthur comes forward and claps his hands)*

Arthur: Drink up everybody. The hearse has arrived. Elsie dear, if you'd like to clear the glasses off your Uncle George, we'll get under way. Minnie, give him a quick rub over with the Mansion House, will you. *(Elsie clears the glasses and bottles off the coffin and Minnie polishes the lid)* Right, pallbearers, please. The four god-children, I think. That would be nice, he always enjoyed young people's company.

> *(Harold, Jeffrey, and two other cousins step forward. They lift the coffin on to their shoulders)*

Arthur: That's the style. Right . . . off we go. Nice and steady. Don't drop him.

(They walk towards the door. The door opens and Potty Aida is standing there. A woman of sixty dressed as a twenty-year-old in 1940 – à la Rita Hayworth. She is over-made up to the point of ghastliness)

Aida: Ah, caught you! Bleeding going without me, weren't you?

Arthur: No, Aida dear, we weren't going without you.

Aida: Oh yes you bleeding well were.

Arthur: No, we weren't, Aida. Now, remember, this is a funeral, we don't want any swearing.

Aida: You call that bleeding swearing – you wait till we get to the cemetery.

Arthur: Now Aida, please, we don't want any scenes this time.

Minnie: If she's going, make sure she's got her knickers on.

Aida: You mind your own business. I've got me drawers on so don't you worry. They don't come off as often as yours.

Minnie: What do you mean by that?

Aida: What do I mean? You had a lovely bleeding war, didn't you? All them Canadians.

Caroline: I'll look after her, don't worry. Come on, Auntie Aida.

Arthur: Come along, everybody, we'll be late.

First woman: What about Uncle Nobby?

Second woman: I'll get him.

Joyce: For gawd's sake, keep him away from the hole.

(The women pick up the wreaths and pallbearers go out into the hallway with the coffin. We hear bangs as they bump into the furniture in the hall. We hear them calling to each other. 'Mind the hall-stand'. 'Left hand down a bit'. 'Up your end, Harold'. The rest of the family file out behind them. The last one to leave is Albert, still wearing his bowler hat).

SCENE 7

All the cars come roaring out of the cemetery and race down the road, overtaking each other. They come tearing round the corner and screech to a halt outside Uncle George's house. The family pile out and rush into the house as fast as they can.

Harold's car draws up sedately; he hasn't bothered to join in the gold rush. He and Albert get out. Albert gestures to Harold to hurry up.

SCENE 8

Uncle George's front room. The family are standing there, looking round aghast. The whole room is empty. Every piece of furniture, every painting, every ornament has gone. The room is denuded. Albert comes in, followed by Harold.

Albert: What's happened?

Arthur: We've been burgled. There's nothing here.

Alice: *(entering)* There's nothing upstairs, either. The linen cupboard's empty as well.

(Jessie and Joyce run in)

Jessie: They've cleaned out the front room!

Joyce: There's not a stick left.

(Harold starts laughing)

Arthur: I see nothing to laugh at.

Harold: Don't you. I thinks it's hysterical. They must have had a furniture van waiting round the corner. Oh dear, it's made my day, this has.

Arthur: Jeffrey, go and get the police.

(The young man leaves)

Old man: What about the will? They haven't nicked that as well?

Arthur: I've got the will.

Minnie: Thank gawd for that, we still might get something out of it.

Jessie: Go on, then, read it. How much has he left?

Harold: *(to Arthur)* Let's get out of here, we don't want to listen to this.

Albert: No, I'm stopping, mate. I want my twenty-five quid back I lent him.

(Arthur takes out an envelope and opens it, takes out the will)

Arthur: The last will and testament of George Nightingale Steptoe ... *(He opens the will and reads)* 'I, George Nightingale Steptoe, being of sound body and mind. . .'

Albert: Blimey, he must have wrote that in 1923.

Arthur: ... 'do hereby make my last will and testament. To the Steptoe family –' *(they all mutter eagerly)* – 'if everything has gone according to plan you are now standing in an empty house. You are no doubt wondering where everything has gone. Well, I've sold it. I arranged for it to be collected while you were at the funeral so that none of you greedy so-and-sos could get your thieving hands on it. The money I got for it along with the rest of my estate, amounting to fifteen hundred and twenty-seven

pounds, I divide equally between ...' (*they all lean forward eagerly*) '... the RSPCA and the Battersea Dogs' Home. You'll find a tray of drinks already poured out to help you get over the shock. Good luck and see you all soon.'

There is consternation. They all start arguing amongst themselves. Harold takes a glass from a tray on a packing case. He is delighted)

Harold: Ladies and gentlemen, please – quiet, please. On this very solemn occasion, may I propose a toast? Will you please charge your glasses and drink to the memory of George Nightingale, the first Steptoe I've ever known with a sense of humour.

Arthur: Never, I wouldn't touch it. After all I've done for him!

Aida: He was always bleeding vindictive.

Joyce: I've never been so insulted in all my life.

Minnie: It's disgraceful. I won't stay in this house another minute.

(They all start leaving, furious at the injustice of it all)

Alice: Well, you'll never see me at the graveside. I'm telling you.

Elsie: I never thought he'd do this to me. I looked after him like a daughter.

Joyce: When I think of the money I spent on bus fares coming round to see him.

Jessie: I wasn't expecting anything for myself, but you'd have thought he'd leave his granddaughter something.

Nobby: *(drunk)* The wages of sin are death. We're all doomed.

(The room empties, leaving just Harold and Albert with the tray of drinks)

Harold: I enjoyed that. It was worth coming, after all. You're not upset, are you Dad?

Albert: Me? No. I thought he'd do something like that.

Harold: Are you going to drink to him?

Albert: Might as well. Shame to waste it.

Harold: To Uncle George.

Albert: To George.

Harold: Well, take your hat off, Dad, show a bit of respect.

(Albert takes his bowler hat off. Perched on his head is the porcelain group. He removes it from his head. Harold stares at him)

Harold: You crafty old devil. Steptoe the klepto!

Albert: Must be worth the twenty-five quid he owed me. *(Albert raises his glass and looks up to heaven)* Better luck next time, George.

(Harold and Albert drink, then take two more glasses from the tray).

Live Now, P.A.Y.E. Later

First transmission 13 March 1972

Live Now, P.A.Y.E. Later featured
Colin Gordon as The Tax Inspector with Edwin Apps and Peter
Madden and was produced by John Howard Davies

SCENE 1
The Steptoes' yard. There is banging coming from inside a
wardrobe. It is shaking. The door bursts open and Albert falls
out, cursing. He slams the door shut and angrily pushes the
wardrobe over. He goes into the house.

SCENE 2
The outside of a house. The horse and cart are waiting. Harold
comes out of the house carrying a sack. A woman half opens the
door in her underwear. She looks nervously up and down the
street to see if the neighbours are watching. She calls to Harold.
Harold is halfway down the path. He turns. She points to the
sack. He looks round, hurries back to the doorstep, opens the
sack, takes out a blouse and skirt and gives them to her. He
touches his cap. She goes back in and Harold gets on the cart and
drives off.

SCENE 3
The Steptoes' lounge. Albert is laying the table. Harold enters
carrying the sack of clothes.

Harold: Another five million sacks like these and we can retire.
 Where do you fancy? The South of France? Good afternoon,
 Father.
Albert: What's good about it?
Harold: Oh, there's no doubt about it, you can't beat the joys of

65

living at home. The cheerful welcome at the gate, the sunny smile of pleasure as his kindly old face lights up at the pleasure of seeing his son again, the warm glow of a roaring fire in the grate, the delicious smell of the dinner wafting in from the kitchen *(waggles his fingers)*, disappearing up your hooter and transporting you into a heady euphoric trance of mouthwatering anticipation. *(Closes his eyes)* Just like one of the Bisto kids. Ah! Ah! What have we got?

Albert: A tin of sardines.

Harold: Thank you, the Galloping Gourmet. You said you were making a steak and kidney pudding today.

Albert: I haven't had time.

Harold: Haven't had time? You've had all day.

Albert: I've been out in the yard all day, locked in that bleeding wardrobe.

Harold: And what, pray, were you doing in the wardrobe?

Albert: I was woodworming it.

Harold: And how were you doing that? Crawling down the holes hitting them with little hammers?

Albert: Very funny. I bought a tin of stuff, didn't I? Out of my own money. I was inside painting it on, and somebody locked the door.

Harold: I know who it was.

Albert: Who?

Harold: Superworm. The King of the Woodwork. With one mighty flick of his tail the door was shut, and clumping his steel-like choppers over the key, he spun in the air like a Catherine wheel, incarcerating his mortal enemy in a living tomb.

Albert: How would you like a tin of sardines round your ear'ole? *(He empties the tin of sardines on a plate)*

Albert: Get that down you.

Harold: No. No. I couldn't. I couldn't eat another mouthful. I'm full up. I had a bag of crisps at lunchtime.

Albert: Do you want them or not?

Harold: No, I don't.

(Albert tips them on his own plate and gets stuck into them)

Harold: I shall jump into my howdah, and go down to the Indian restaurant for a Tandoori special. *(He picks up a pile of letters from the table and sifts through them)*

Albert: What have you got in the sack?

Harold: Mixed rags. Some cream, some dark. Couple of dresses, blouses, a few hats. Bought them off a bird whose granny died. I'll sort them out later. Hello, Inland Revenue. Mr A. Steptoe. Personal. What do they want with you, you haven't paid any income tax for years. You told them you didn't want to join, didn't you?

Albert: Show us. (*Harold hands him the envelope. Albert opens it and reads the letter. His face drops as he reads. He is very worried*) Oh my gawd.

Harold: What's the matter? (*Albert hands him the letter. Harold reads it*) 'Dear sir, one of our Inspectors will be calling on you in regard to a discrepancy in your income tax returns. The query is in respect of the allowance claimed for your wife. We should be grateful if . . .' What wife?

Albert: I've been claiming for your mother.

Harold: She's been dead thirty-three years!

Albert: I know. I never told them.

Harold: And you've been claiming for her all this time?

Albert: Yeah. Well, you save forty quid a year. The first year I put her down by mistake, and they never said anything, so I've been putting her down ever since. Harold, what will they do?

Harold: Well, you for a start. Dad, this is a very serious offence. It's deliberate fraud. They can fine you up to ten times the amount you've fiddled them out of.

Albert: I haven't got that sort of money.

Harold: Then it's up to two years inside.

Albert: (*horrified*) Prison?

Harold: Well, I don't think it'll be a nudist colony.

Albert: Harold, I can't do porridge at my time of life. I'll never come out.

Harold: You're lucky you're living in this country. If you were living in Saudi Arabia, they'd chop your hands off. In the Sudan they chop your whatsits off. Or both. Of course, you'll have to send your medals back, and resign from the British Legion.

Albert: You're enjoying this, aren't you?

Harold: Well, what a stupid thing to do. You risk everything for a few quid a year. You never get away with defrauding the Inland Revenue. They always get you in the end. They've got nothing else to do.

Albert: I'm sorry, Harold. I won't do it again. What am I going to do?

Harold: I don't know. You could plead insanity – yeah, that's it. You've never accepted your wife's death. You still think she's alive. You still talk to her. You set a place for her at the dinner table. You send her birthday cards.

Albert: They'll put me in a nut-house.

Harold: It's up to you. Eighteen months in the nick or the rest of your life in a nut-house.

Albert: Oh gawd, I don't know what to do. When's he coming?

Harold: (*looking at the letter*) This afternoon.

Albert: What time?

Harold: Half past four.

Albert: What's the time now?

Harold: (*looks at his watch*) Half past four.

> (*There is a loud knock at the door. Albert nearly has a heart attack. He clutches Harold*)

Albert: Don't let them take me, Harold, please don't let them take me.

Harold: All right, now keep calm. Just sit down, relax. Don't commit yourself. Try and look honest.

Albert: Oh gawd!

Harold: Play the old soldier. Put your medals on. Where's that photograph of Ted Heath?

Albert: You smashed it.

Harold: Well, where's the one of the Queen? Put that up.

> (*Harold goes out of the room. Albert frantically fumbles through a drawer, finds a presentation box. He opens it, takes out a row of medals and clips it on his jacket*)

SCENE 4

The hall. Harold opens the front door. The Income Tax Inspector is standing there carrying a briefcase.

Inspector: Good afternoon.

Harold: Good afternoon.

Inspector: My name is Greenwood. Inland Revenue.

Harold: Ah yes, you must be the gentleman they wrote to my father about.

Inspector: That's right. Are your parents in?

Harold: Well, my father is in, he's waiting for you.

Inspector: And your mother?

Harold: Well, she's waiting for him . . . that is to say, she's expecting him any time now . . . I mean . . . she's not here . . . she's sleeping.

Inspector: Would it be inconvenient to wake her up?

Harold: Not so much inconvenient . . . as . . . difficult. You see . . .

Inspector: Well, it doesn't matter. I'm sure your father can answer all the questions I have in mind.

Harold: Yes, won't you come in?

Inspector: Thank you.

(The Inspector comes in the hallway. Harold closes the door)

Harold: I think I ought to warn you, he's getting on a bit. His mind isn't what it was. He's a bit vague, hazy, tends to ramble a bit, fantasizes things. I wouldn't put too much credence on what he says. He's a bit senile.

Inspector: Yes. It's quite straightforward.

Harold: It was the '14–'18 war, you know. He never came out of it the way he went in. He was intact . . . physically, except for his teeth. But up here *(taps his head)* . . . it's been a great struggle for us all.

Inspector: I'm terribly sorry. Did he get a disability pension? Only he hasn't entered it on his tax returns.

Harold: *(quickly)* No, no, he didn't. They were very hard in those days. If you finished up in one piece that's all they worried about. He's got medals. For King and Country, it says. A lot of good they did him.

Inspector: Yes, very sad. You'll find Government departments these days are much more humane and understanding.

Harold: Oh, that is good news. He's in here.

SCENE 5

The lounge. Albert is sitting there petrified. His hands are shaking. There is a picture of the Queen on the wall, decked in the Union Jack.

Harold: *(entering)* Father, this is Mr Greenwood from the Inland Revenue.

Inspector: Good afternoon, Mr Steptoe.

Albert: *(coming to attention and saluting)* How do you do, sir.

Harold: At ease, Dad. Mr Greenwood has one or two questions to ask you.

Inspector: I'll be as brief as I can. I'm sure we can clear it all up in no time.

Harold: Please sit down.

Inspector: Thank you. Er . . . *(looks at Albert)*

Harold: Sit down, Dad.

(The Inspector sits down and takes a file out of his briefcase)

Harold: May I get you a drink?

Inspector: Oh, thank you. A cup of tea would be nice.

Harold: Oh, come now, something a little stronger in this cold weather?

Inspector: That is kind of you. If you're having one.

Harold: Yes, yes, we'll join you.

(Harold pours two Scotches in spirit glasses, then takes a half pint beer mug and fills it half full with Scotch)

Inspector: Ah. Pip, Squeak and Wilfred I see!

Harold: Soda?

Inspector: Thank you.

(Harold squirts a tiny drop of soda in the glass and hands it to the Inspector)

Harold: Cheers.

Inspector: Your very good health. *(Drinks)* It's not often I can afford the luxury of spirits on my income.

Harold: Yes, well, of course, neither can we. This is in fact what's left of a Christmas present from someone in the trade.

Inspector: Well now *(he opens the file)*, let's get straight to the point . . .

Harold: *(moving the plate of sardines)* Excuse me, our dinner. *(He pats Albert's shoulder)* Never mind, Dad, it's Friday tomorrow, we'll have a bit of meat. *(To Inspector)* Cheers.

Inspector: Oh yes, cheers *(He drinks again)* The point in question, Mr Steptoe, is the allowance you have been claiming for your wife.

Albert: Cheers.

Inspector: Cheers, yes. *(He drinks again)*

Albert: They used to give this when we were going over the top. Tanked us right up, they did. Had to. Couldn't face it otherwise. All my platoon were wiped out before we got ten yards.

Inspector: Yes, it was shocking. Now, about your wife . . .

Albert: Butchers, our generals were. The Germans were crying over their machine guns, they were, as they were wiping us out.

Inspector: Dear me. Here, for instance, you have claimed the full marriage allowance and . . .

Harold: Cheers.

Inspector: Cheers. *(He drinks)*

Albert: Lions led by donkeys, we were. I never want to go through that again.

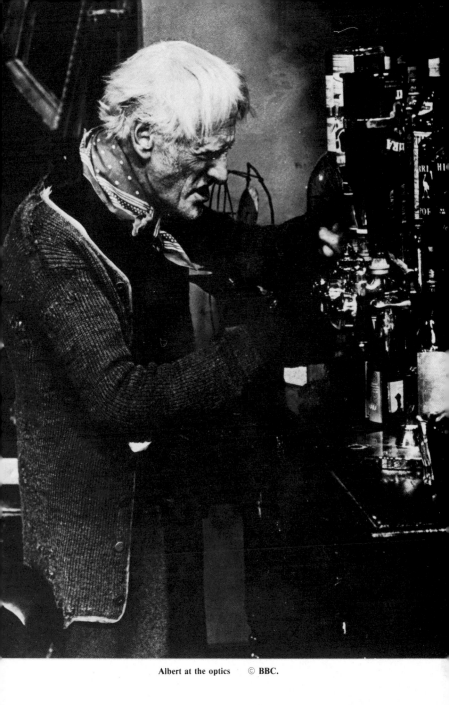

Albert at the optics   © **BBC.**

Alan Simpson (left) and Ray Galton (right),
the creators of Steptoe and Son, with the producer, Duncan Wood, in the series' early days

Part of the programme's fascination lay in the glimpses given of an
intriguing array of clutter which — careful viewers maintain — had
constantly changing details around focal points such as the skeleton

Another of the many treasures of the Steptoe household © BBC

Filming for 'Steptoe': Harry H. Corbett and Wilfred Brambell are on the cart, the lighting man from the film camera crew rides the horse, which is led by its owner, Arthur Arnold, while film cameraman John McGlashan is roped to the cart and producer Duncan Wood walks alongside © BBC

Albert and Harold with Hercules © BBC

'Cuckoo in the Nest': Harold discovers he has a half-brother, Arthur
(played by Kenneth J. Warren), from the other side of the world

Galton and Simpson had now been writing the series for almost ten years...

The Albert Steptoe they had created was proud of having fought in the First World War, so proud that he gave his son the embarrassing middle name of 'Kitchener' © BBC

'Oh What a Beautiful Morning', Harold and Albert are left alone after the funeral — and Albert keeps his secret under his hat   Don Smith © BBC

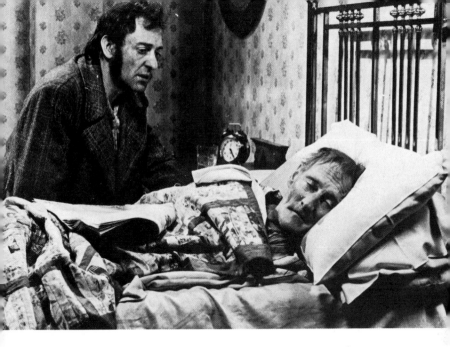

Albert was never ashamed of using emotional blackmail against Harold, or of upstaging him — as he did in 'A Star is Born'

© BBC

Harold and Albert preparing their feast for 'Christmas 1973', which featured a larger cast than usual. Here are some the camera never saw; the wardrobe and make-up staff, camera and sound crews, lighting and technical operations staff, the electrical and scene crews and the production unit behind the stars

© BBC

One of the recurring themes of the show, as in 'And So To Bed', was the thwarting of Harold's amorous intentions   Don Smith, © BBC

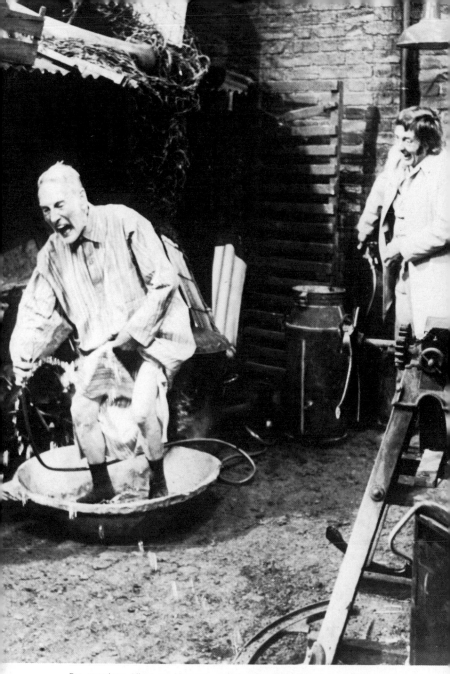

But sometimes Albert got his come-uppance. Here Harold watches in delight as his malingering father, who has had him running 'Upstairs, Downstairs, Upstairs, Downstairs' tries to wash away the effects of a too-vigorous spirit rub

Don Smith, © BBC

Inspector: No indeed, let's hope no one ever has to.

Harold: I'll drink to that. Peace and prosperity to us all.

Inspector: *(the drink taking effect)* Yes, preace and posperity to us all. *(They all drink)*

Inspector: *(clears throat)* Now . . . you were married in 1918.

Albert: Yes, I came home on leave. I had a Blighty wound. I had a piece of shrapnel up my arras.

Inspector: Painful . . .

Harold: He's never been the same man.

Inspector: And you've claimed the marriage allowance ever since.

Harold: Yes, well, we can explain that . . .

Inspector: Yes?
(Pause)

Albert: I used to have black-outs. I didn't know what I was doing.

Harold: Cheers.

Inspector: Oh . . . cheers. *(He drinks again)* When was your wife born, Mr Stoetep? Er . . . Steptoe. *(He is slightly drunk now)*

Albert: 1901.

Inspector: Exactly. 1901. That's what we have here. And so she is now seventy-one years old. She has been an old-age pensioner for six years.

Albert: Yes, well . . .

Inspector: And yet you have never entered her pension on your Income Tax returns. That is a very serious omission.

Harold: Hang on a minute . . .

Inspector: Cheers.

Harold: Eh? Oh . . . cheers.
(They drink again)

Inspector: *(more drunk)* The law says every source of income must be declared on your returns. Without exception. That is very remiss of you. Very naughty.

Albert: *(outraged)* I've never drawn her pension.

Inspector: I beg your pardon? Not drawn her pension? Oh dear, oh dear. Oh dear me. We can't have that. Why ever not? It's hard enough for the old folk to manage as it is. Mrs Steptoe must have her pension. I shall speak to the Ministry of Health and Social Security. You're so proud, you old people, it's so silly. Sardines for lunch, oh, no no. Your mother is entitled to a pension. The wife of an old soldier – it's disgraceful. *(He is now more drunk)* I shall personally see that she gets every penny she's entitled to. I'll see she gets it retro . . . retrospectable . . . recto . . .

Harold: Retrospectively.

Inspector: Thank you. Yes. Six years at – ooh . . . um . . . er . . . that's hundreds of pounds . . .

Albert: How much?

Inspector: Over a thousand, I should think. They can afford it. Look at the surplus they've got. Hundreds of millions. What's the point of having a surplus if the poor little old lady is not getting her pension? They'll only spend it on the Concorde or some other daft bloody thing. Not another word. (*He lurches to his feet with his glass*) I shall speak to the Ministry myself. There'll be a man round here first thing in the morning. She can use the money to get a decent home. Look at this place. Old people shouldn't have to live in a place like this. Mrs Steptoe will just have to sign a form and that's all there is to it. (*He drains his glass. He is now very drunk*) You're to leave everything to me. I shall now bid you good afternoon. (*He has a job putting his things back in the briefcase. He tries to salute Albert*) I salute you, sir. Tell Mrs Steptoe not to worry about a thing. Good day, sir. (*He stumbles and almost falls. Harold supports him and helps him out of the room. Inspector sings drunkenly*) 'I shall not cease from mental strife. Nor shall my sword sleep in my hand. Till we have built Jerusalem. In England's green and pleasant land.'

SCENE 6
The yard. Harold is seeing the Inspector off.

Harold: Have you got far to go?

Inspector: No, it's all right, I've got my car outside. Up the workers!
　　(*He lurches off across the yard. Harold shuts the door*)

SCENE 7
The lounge.

Albert: That's all right, ain't it? A thousand quid.

Harold: No, it's not all right. Compounding a felony, this is. Double bumble. Five years now. (*Albert is frightened again. He drinks*) That's it, go on, get drunk. You might as well, while you've got the chance. The only bars they've got in the place you're going are across the windows.
　　(*Albert looks terrified*)

SCENE 8

The hall. It is the next morning. There is a knock on the door. Harold comes out and opens it. The man from the Ministry of Health and Social Security is standing there.

Man: Good morning. I'm from the Ministry of Health and Social Security. I'd like to speak to Mrs Steptoe.

Harold: Yes. I think you'd better come in.

SCENE 9

The lounge. Harold ushers the man in and closes the door.

Man: Is Mrs Steptoe at home?

Harold: Look, we can't let this go on any longer.

Man: I quite agree. It's a very lamentable oversight on our part. Never mind, I've got the cheque for the six years' arrears. If you wouldn't mind telling Mrs Steptoe I'm here, we'll just get her to sign the appropriate forms, I'll give her her pension book, and away she goes.

Harold: Yeah, where? Look, I'm afraid it's not quite as ... would you care for a drink? Scotch, gin, vodka?

Man: No, thank you. I don't drink.

Harold: Oh. Look, I may as well be perfectly frank with you ... I'm afraid my mother ...

(The door opens and Albert comes in dressed up as a woman of seventy – complete with wig and hat. Harold reacts)

Albert: I'm just going down the shops, Harold. What would you like for tea? Oh – you've got company.

Man: Mrs Steptoe?

Albert: Yes.

Man: Mrs Gladys Steptoe?

Albert: Yes.

(Harold sits)

Man: I cannot apologize enough for this dreadful mistake. But rest assured, we'll soon put it right.

Harold: Look, Mother, why don't you go down the shops and let me sort this out?

Albert: Why don't you mind your own business, your mother knows what she's doing.

Harold: I know what she'll be doing if she gets caught. *(The man* *looks sharply at him*) By my father, that is. You know he doesn't like you signing things when he's not here. Why don't you go and get him?

Albert: I can sign anything I like, I don't have to ask his permission.

Man: As you wish. (*He opens his case and takes out a form*) There you are. If you would just sign there.

(*Albert takes pen in his right hand*)

Albert: Gladys . . . Mary . . . Steptoe.

Man: (*taking the form*) That's fine. (*He hands Albert a cheque*) And here is a cheque for eleven hundred and fifty-three pounds back pension . . . and here is your new pension book, starting from this week. And long may you live to spend it.

Albert: Thanks ever so.

Man: Well, that's it, then. I won't bother you any longer. I'm sorry I missed Mr Steptoe. (*He rises and shakes hands with Albert*)

Harold: Oh come along, Mother, where's your gratitude? Don't just shake hands, I think he deserves a little kiss. It's not every day you get a cheque for eleven hundred pounds. Go on, kiss the kind gentleman.

(*Albert glowers at him and then gives the man a peck on the cheek. The man laughs and kisses Albert on the cheek*)

Man: Goodbye, my dear. Look after yourself.

SCENE 10
The hall. Harold is ushering the man out.

Man: A very unusual woman, your mother.

Harold: You don't know how unusual.

Man: She certainly seems to have something other women don't.

Harold: Oh, she has, she has.

Man: Goodbye. Take care of her.

Harold: Don't worry, I'll take care of her. (*The man leaves. Harold closes the door*) Right now. (*He storms into the lounge*)

SCENE 11
The lounge.

Harold: You've done it now, haven't you? Of all the stupid things to do!

Albert: What's the matter with you?

Harold: And take that silly hat and wig off. You look like Old Mother Riley. How long do you think you'll be able to carry on this ludicrous masquerade?

Albert: As long as I have to. Shouldn't be difficult. I'll have to dress up once a week to go and draw my pension, that's all. (*Albert lifts his skirt up to reveal long peach-coloured elastic bloomers. He eases his finger round the leg elastic*) Gorblimey, this elastic don't half cut into your legs.

Harold: You haven't gone funny, have you? What are you wearing them for?

Albert: I'm not going up the stairs on the bus without them, mate, I'm telling you.

Harold: You won't get away with it, you know. One day you'll forget to put them on. The conductor'll catch you. And you'll both end up inside.

(*Albert looks worried*)

SCENE 12

Albert, wearing different women's clothes and looking very smart, is getting off a bus, assisted by the conductor. He goes into a post office.

SCENE 13

Inside the post office. There is a queue of old people at the pension counter. Albert joins the end of the queue. An old man joins behind Albert. The queue moves up. Albert jumps as the old man gooses him. Albert turns round. The old man winks at him.

Old man: Hello, dearie.

Albert: Are you asking for a clout round the ear'ole?

Old man: Oh ho, that's what I like, a bit of spirit. What's your name, love?

Albert: Mind your own business.

(*The old man looks at Albert's pension book which he is holding in his hand*)

Old man: Gladys . . . that's a nice name. It suits you. I'm Norman. How do you do. (*He goes as if to shake hands but at the last minute pinches Albert's backside*)

Albert: If you do that again, mush, I'll . . . I'll . . .

Old man: You'll what?

Albert: I'll call a policeman.

Old man: I am a policeman. At least I was. I'm retired.

Albert: Oh well, it's been very nice . . . *(he makes as if to leave)*

Old man: No, no, you haven't drawn your money yet. There's only one in front of you, you won't be long. Yes, I was a sergeant. In the fraud squad.

Albert: Oh gawd.

Old man: Yes, you'd be surprised at the swindles people get up to. Not much got past me, though. I can spot phoneys a mile away. I always know when they're on the fiddle. *(It's Albert's turn at the counter. He passes his book over)* Relentless, I was. Never gave up. Once I got my teeth into a case, that was it. I always got them in the end. *(The clerk passes Albert his money. Albert hurries to get away. The old man clutches his arm)* Not so fast. I want a word with you. *(Albert is almost ready to faint. The old man hands his book over the counter)* What are you doing this afternoon?

Albert: Eh?

Old man: Fancy coming to the pictures?

Albert: I can't. I've got to get my son's dinner ready.

Old man: He must be big enough to get his own. We can get in for a bob each. My treat. If you're nice I might even give you a hot dog.

Albert: *(trying to get away)* I can't.

Old man: It's a good programme: *What Are You Doing After The Orgy?*

Albert: Pardon?

Old man: That's the title. And *Wife Swapping, French Style*.

Albert: No, I don't like those sort of films. And I'm not that sort of girl. If you'll excuse me.

(The old man lets go of Albert's arms in order to collect his pension book. Albert seizes the opportunity to get away)

Old man: I'll meet you outside.

SCENE 14

Albert comes out of the post office, looks up and down, and runs up the street. His shoe comes off. The old man comes out and looks up and down. He sees the shoe and picks it up. He hurries away in the same direction.

Albert arrives at a Ladies' and Gents' convenience. He goes

straight down the gents' side. There is a pause. He comes running back up followed by an irate attendant.

The old man arrives just as Albert re-emerges. Albert bumps into him. He offers Albert his shoe.

Old man: *(seductively)* Hello, Cinders.

SCENE 15

The back row of the cinema. Albert is sitting unhappily next to the old man. The old man slides his arm round Albert's shoulders. Albert edges away. The old man's hand comes to rest on Albert's chest. Albert freezes in horror.

SCENE 16

A Darby and Joan Club. The last waltz is in progress. Albert is dancing with the old man. The old man is singing into Albert's ear.

Old man: 'Who's taking you home tonight, After the dance is through. Who's the lucky boy that's going your way, To kiss you goodnight at your doorway . . .'

SCENE 17

The yard. It is dark. Albert comes running into the yard. He looks up and down the street. His clothes are awry – hat on the side of his head, blouse open, torn, etc. He decides he is safe. He totters over to the front door and goes in.

SCENE 18

The lounge. Albert comes in and crosses to drinks. Harold is sitting there in his dressing-gown.

Harold: Where the bleeding hell have you – Gordon Bennett, what's happened to you? Somebody tried to have a go?
Albert: Yeah. A dirty old ex-copper. He fancies me.
Harold: An ex-copper? Well . . . you could do a lot worse, Mother.
Albert: It's no joke. I think he wants to marry me.

Harold: Well, I'm not surprised, you are a very attractive woman.

Albert: Oh, cobblers. *(Harold laughs)* Fraud squad, he said. If he picks me up in the post office again it's only a matter of time before he finds out. *(He takes his wig off and throws it on to the table. He takes his blouse off, revealing a large brassière stuffed to overflowing with paper, cotton wool, etc)* What am I going to do, Harold?

Harold: I'll tell you what you are going to do. You're going to send all the money back now.

Albert: Eh?

Harold: Anonymously.

Albert: What about the pension? That's got to be drawn every week.

Harold: Not if you do what I say. *(He puts a pad and pen in front of Albert)* Write the following. 'Dear sir, it is with great regret that I have to inform you . . .'

(Fade on Albert writing to Harold's dictation)

SCENE 19

The lounge. Harold brings mail in. Albert is there, now dressed normally. Harold hands him a letter.

Harold: It's for you, the Inland Revenue.

Albert: *(opens the letter and reads)* 'Dear Mr Steptoe, I was very sad indeed to hear of the tragic death of your wife.'

Harold: See, it worked, you're in the clear.

Albert: *(sadly)* There's more. *(He hands the letter to Harold)*

Harold: 'However, before we close her file, there is the question of death duties to clear up. I assume she will have left her estate to be shared between you, your son and your daughter. In which case it will' – what daughter?

Albert: Muriel.

Harold: Who's Muriel?

Albert: My daughter, the one I've been claiming for. She's thirty-five.

Harold: You can't claim for a daughter of thirty-five.

Albert: She works for me. She's my secretary. I pay her twelve quid a week.

Harold: I give up. I get you out of one hole and you go and dig another one.

Albert: He says it's only a formality. Mr Greenwood will just want her signature. He says to save time he'll come round and see Muriel personally. Harold . . .

Harold: Oh no. Oh no, not me.

Albert: It'll only be the once. I'll give her the sack tomorrow.

Harold: No. Under no circumstances. I will not do it. I'm not interested. This time you can go to the nick and it won't be Holloway.

SCENE 20
The yard. Mr Greenwood, the Tax Inspector, is knocking at the front door. Albert opens the door. He is in mourning.

Albert: Mr Greenwood, how nice to see you again. Come in.

Inspector: I'm so sorry about your dear wife.

Albert: Yes, yes, a great shock to us all. She didn't suffer.

Inspector: Good. Good. This won't take long.

SCENE 21
The lounge. Albert and the Tax Inspector enter.

Albert: Would you like a drink?

Inspector: Er . . . no, no, I don't think I'd better. I'll just get your three signatures and I'll be off.

Albert: Well, Harold's out on the round, but Muriel's here. I'll call her. *(Calls from door)* Muriel.

Inspector: Children can be very comforting for a man at a time like this.

Albert: Oh yes. She's a good girl.

(The door opens and Harold enters in a sophisticated black dress, string of pearls, wig and make-up, and holding a lace hankie, with which he dabs his eyes)

Harold: You called, Father?

Albert: This is Mr Greenwood from the Inland Revenue.

Inspector: *(instantly smitten; he rises and takes Harold's hand)* Allow me to offer my condolences, Miss Steptoe. I almost feel as if I knew your mother personally. *(Harold sniffs and dabs his eyes)* There, there, courage, my dear. Don't give way. This won't take long. Just your signature. *(He gets out a form from his case)*

Albert: Well . . . if you will excuse me, I'll leave you two together. I'll just pop out and see what's happened to Harold.

(Albert leaves the room. The Inspector sits down next to Harold. Harold edges away. The Inspector starts going over the documents, trying to get as close as he can to Harold as he explains what they mean . . .)

Loathe Story

First transmission 20 March 1972

Loathe Story featured
Raymond Huntley as The Psychiatrist
with Georgina Cookson and Joanna Lumley
and was produced by John Howard Davies

SCENE 1

The Steptoes' yard, where a badminton court has been set up.
Harold and Albert are playing. Harold is in full Wimbledon gear –
sweat-band on wrist, etc. Albert is in his working clothes and hat.
Harold is dancing about waiting for the old man to serve. He does
so. Harold misses the shuttlecock completely.
   Albert serves again. Harold falls over in a vain attempt to return
the shuttlecock.
   Albert serves again. Harold misses it again. They walk over to a
table by the net where there are bottles of glucose, a stack of
plastic beakers and a water urn – just like Wimbledon. Harold
throws his racket on the table and wipes his forehead with the
towel. He pours a little glucose into his cup, fills it up from the
urn, drinks some, swills the rest round his mouth and spits it out.
Albert drinks his right down.
   Harold pours some resin on his hand, rubs his hand up and
down his racket handle, and takes up his position on court. Albert
picks up his racket and takes up his position. They have now
changed ends.

Albert: Your service.
   (*Harold carefully prepares to serve. He tosses the shuttlecock in the
   air and misses it. He picks it up and tries again. This time he hits it
   either into the net or out of court*)
Albert: Game set and match. (*He scampers over to Harold to shake
   hands. Harold ignores him and walks over to the table. He slings his
   racket away in anger. Albert joins him and pours himself a drink while*

Harold wipes himself down) I thought you said you could play this game. *(Harold ignores him. He puts his rackets in their Dunlop covers)* How long have you been having lessons? *(Harold ignores him)* Waste of money, however long it is. All that gear must have set you back a few bob as well. If I was you I'd cut your losses and flog it all.

Harold: Have you finished?

Albert: Well, it's a laugh. You're always the same. Taking up things, buying all the gear, spending all your money, and then you're a scrub-out.

Harold: If you don't shut up, I'll take this shuttlecock, I shall run it straight up your Khyber and set fire to the feathers. In any case I'm not taking this seriously. Shuttlecock – this is just a limber up, to loosen my muscles. Tennis is my game. You can't play tennis out here, on a titchy pitch like this.

Albert: Court.

Harold: I know the terminology.

Albert: That's about all you do know – you can't play.

Harold: How can I play properly out here! Sliding about on the horse manure.

Albert: It was the same for me.

Harold: You've got hob-nailed boots on.

Albert: You could have put your boots on.

Harold: Don't be ridiculous, not with this gear. You wouldn't expect to see Princess Anne wearing frogman's flippers when she's show-jumping, would you?

Albert: Do you fancy another game?

Harold: No.

Albert: We won't score this time, then you won't know how many I've beaten you by.

Harold: I don't want to play any more.

Albert: Well, put my name down for the tennis club, I'll give you a clobbering down there.

Harold: So help me, if you so much as set foot in that tennis club, I'll murder you. I've made some very nice friends down there, a very nice class of person. You stay away from there. They're very refined people down there. They don't want any dirty, smelly, uncouth little foul-mouthed shitehawks in hob-nailed boots churning up their lawns. Now, if you'll excuse me, I am going to take a shower and get an early night. *(He picks up his racket, towels, etc. and walks over to the house)*

Albert: You can't stop me joining. They'd be glad to have me.

Harold: Huh!

Albert: Coaching them, if they're as bad as you. I was champion of my regiment . . .

Harold: (*at the door*) I know you were. You were champion of everything, weren't you? You were a one-man Olympic team you were, weren't you? I don't know why you don't go to bleeding Munich. Walk in carrying the flag all on your own. Eight hundred Russians, nine hundred Americans, and you. (*Mimics Albert*) Sorry I'm out of breath. I've just brought the torch up from Athens. What shall I do first? The decathlon or the three mile steeplechase? (*Own voice*) You stay away from that tennis club. All right? (*He goes in and closes the door*)

Albert: (*shouts*) Just because you know I'll beat you. I always beat you. Because you're a scrub-out. You're useless. You're a pudden.

(*The door opens and Harold pelts him with tennis balls*)

SCENE 2
Harold's bedroom. Harold is in bed asleep, having a nightmare. He is tossing and turning.

Harold: (*mimics old man*) I've beat you. Game set and match. Beat you. Snap. Beat you. Down the snake you go. Hotel on Mayfair. Two thousand pounds. Beat you. Checkmate. Beat you. Full house. Beat you. Beat you. Beat you. Beat you.

(*Harold quietens down and relaxes in his sleep, the nightmare having petered out. Suddenly he sits up in bed, still asleep. He gets out of bed and goes slowly to the door. He is sleep-walking*)

SCENE 3
The landing and stairs. Harold goes out on to the landing and walks down the stairs. He disappears into the lounge. We hear a drawer open and cutlery rattling. There is a pause, then Harold comes out of the lounge carrying a large meat cleaver. He sleep-walks back up the stairs and along the passage to Albert's room. He opens the door and goes in.

SCENE 4

Albert's bedroom. Albert is asleep, snoring. Harold walks over to his bed and stands above him. He raises the meat cleaver above his head and is just about to bring it down on the old man when Albert wakes up. He sees Harold standing over him with the cleaver raised, and screams.

Harold wakes up with a start. The old man carries on screaming. Harold looks bewildered at the cleaver in his hand, and then realizes what he must have been on the verge of doing.

Harold: Oh, my gawd. (*He sinks down on to the bed*)

Albert: (*petrified, pulling the bedclothes up round him*) You're mad! You're potty! You've gone off your nut!

(*Harold lets the cleaver slip out of his hand on to the floor and buries his face in his hands*)

SCENE 5

A psychiatrist's consulting room. The psychiatrist is sitting on a chair next to a couch on which Harold is lying in his working clothes. The psychiatrist has a pad and pencil on his knee.

Psychiatrist: Now just relax, Mr Steptoe, lie back on the couch. I'm just going to ask you a few questions.

(*Harold relaxes and closes his eyes. The psychiatrist takes his hankie and wipes a bit of dirt off the couch where Harold's boots are resting. They are caked with dried mud*)

Psychiatrist: How old are you, Mr Steptoe?

Harold: Thirty-nine.

Psychiatrist: Married?

Harold: No.

Psychiatrist: No?

Harold: No.

Psychiatrist: Oh. Are you homosexual?

Harold: Are you asking for a clout round the earhole?

Psychiatrist: Do you always over-react when your masculinity is questioned?

Harold: I'm not over-reacting. I just don't like being called a brown-hatter, that's all.

Psychiatrist: That's nothing to be ashamed of.

Harold: It is where I come from.

Psychiatrist: It's just that if you were, we might be able to reach a conclusion much quicker than if you try and conceal it.

Harold: I'm not trying to conceal anything. I'm not an iron hoof. I'm a straightforward crumpet man. I've had more grumble than you've had hot dinners.

Psychiatrist: All right, all right, relax. I'm glad to hear it.

(*Harold relaxes again. He crosses his ankles. The psychiatrist, slightly annoyed, again wipes the couch where his boots have been*)

Psychiatrist: Is your mother alive?

Harold: No. She died when I was six.

Psychiatrist: I see. And you have lived alone with your father ever since?

Harold: Yes.

Psychiatrist: And last night you woke up to find yourself standing over him with a meat cleaver in your hand?

Harold: Yeah. I was going to kill him. *(Sits up)* I was going to kill him, my own father.

Psychiatrist: Ah ah ah ah, don't get excited. Lie back, relax. *(He pushes Harold back on to the couch)*

Harold: I was going to kill him – if I hadn't woken up, I would have done him in.

Psychiatrist: That's not necessarily true. You were asleep, you'd had a nightmare. *(He wipes the couch where Harold has rubbed his boots. He is a little more annoyed)* We seldom do things contrary to our natures in these circumstances. They are fantasies we are acting out. I mean, sometimes I dream I'm running down a street, naked.

Harold: Do you?

Psychiatrist: Yes. Don't you?

Harold: No.

Psychiatrist: *(defensively)* Oh. Well, it's a very common dream. I'm surprised you haven't experienced it. I mean, I'm not alone, I assure you. I know many people who . . . er *(coughs)* um . . . Did you love your mother?

Harold: Yes. Yes, I did. Very much.

Psychiatrist: And do you love your father?

Harold: No, I don't.

Psychiatrist: How long have you not liked your father?

Harold: I've never liked him.

Psychiatrist: And have you ever thought about murdering him before?

Harold: Every day – whenever I see him. But I've never tried it.

(The psychiatrist spots some dust on his shoe and wipes it off with his hankie. He leans across to his desk, opens a drawer, takes out a brush. He starts brushing his shoes as Harold carries on talking. The psychiatrist is not listening to him)

Harold: I mean, it's not natural, you can't go round murdering people just because you don't like them. I mean, that's what I'm worried about. I know I was asleep, but I'm frightened it might happen again. One day I might really do it, that's why I've come to you. I want you to help me. *(He stops)*

(There is a pause. The psychiatrist is still brushing his shoes. Harold opens his eyes. He looks at the psychiatrist. The psychiatrist realizes Harold has stopped talking and comes to with a start)

Psychiatrist: Hmm? Oh, carry on. I'm listening.

Harold: Carry on what?

Psychiatrist: Oh. Let me see. *(He puts the brush back in the drawer. We can see a collection of girlie magazines featuring large bosoms)* Um . . . were you rejected as a child?

Harold: Not by my mother.

(The psychiatrist looks at the magazines again, then closes the drawer)

Psychiatrist: Tell me . . . were you breast-fed?

Harold: *(embarrassed)* Well . . . yes, as it happens, I was. Well, we couldn't afford proper milk.

Psychiatrist: *(leans forward, very interested)* Did your mother have a large bosom? Or a small bosom?

Harold: Well . . . it was a fair size, as far as I remember.

Psychiatrist: Large?

Harold: Yeah.

Psychiatrist: Inordinately large . . . or just . . . large?

Harold: Well . . . it seemed quite large at the time . . . I can't be precise, it – what's the size of my mum's bristols got to do with it?

Psychiatrist: I'm just trying to find out whether you miss the security – the comfort – of your mother's bosom. *(Eagerly)* The warm, soft, all-enveloping protection of those two large—

Harold: Hang on, they weren't all that big. Don't you want to know about my father?

Psychiatrist: Hmm? Oh . . . yes, yes all right then. *(Looks at his watch)* Go on then. *(Uninterested)* Unburden your mind. Tell me about your relationship with him. Don't be ashamed. Anything that's lurking in the deepest recesses, winkle it out. None of us are normal, remember that. Go back over the years. Any particular incidents that spring to mind?

Harold: *(closes his eyes again)* Well . . . *(He moves his feet again. The psychiatrist reacts in annoyance. As Harold talks he dusts the couch again)* I suppose one of the earliest memories I have of my father was just before the war. Every night when he came home from work he used to get dressed up and we'd go out on the horse and cart . . .

SCENE 6

Film of Albert as he was at thirty-six – dark haired, a Ronald Colman moustache, upright, his good teeth in, smartly dressed. He is sitting on the horse and cart. Little ten-year-old Harold is sitting next to him, looking miserable.

Harold: (voice over) He used to think he looked like Errol Flynn – silly short-arsed git. Every night we'd go down to the same place. He'd pull up outside the Skinners Arms, go in and leave me outside. *(The horse and cart pulls up outside a pub. Albert gets down and goes in pub)* I used to sit outside there all night with a bottle of lemonade and an arrowroot biscuit. I used to sit there for hours on end. The wind whistled up me gear. Pathetic, it was. Ten years old and I already had a touch of the Farmer Giles. It was disgraceful. *(Little Harold is sitting on the horse and cart with a bottle of lemonade and munching a biscuit)* I wouldn't see him again until chucking out time, then his friends would carry him out, sling him in the back of the cart, and I'd have to take him home. *(Some drunken men carry a dead drunk Albert out of the pub and heave him on to the back of the cart. Little Harold takes the reins and sets off down the road, Albert lying spark out in the back in a drunken stupor)* Night after night that happened. I never got to bed before twelve – up at six to do me paper round. At twelve years old I had bigger bags under my eyes than Harold Macmillan.

   (Film of little Harold in the yard, sitting on stool with a tight-fitting pudding basin on his head coming to just above his ears)

Harold: (voice over) He wouldn't even let me go to the barber's and have a decent haircut. He used to do it himself. *(Albert is cutting round the edge of the basin with a large pair of scissors. Little Harold is in tears as the hair falls off)* I had the worst haircut in the district. The teacher used to let me keep me hat on in class. I was known as Geronimo till I was twenty-three.

SCENE 7
The psychiatrist's consulting room

Harold: When I was eighteen I went into the Army and spent two years fighting in the jungle in Malaya. *(The psychiatrist stifles a yawn and starts doodling on the pad)* I was wounded twice. I caught malaria, foot-rot and three doses of dysentery. That was the happiest two years of my life, 'cos I was away from him. Everything I've ever wanted to do in life he's frustrated, everything I take up he's better at it than I am, but when it comes to the crunch I haven't the heart to beat him. Every time I threaten to leave home he has a heart attack. He's had fifteen heart attacks to my knowledge. (*The psychiatrist is doodling a beautiful girl with enormous bosoms, wielding a whip. He deftly puts the finishing touches to it by indicating her nipples with two little dashes*) I remember one occasion . . . I'd met this girl, we were very keen on each other. At that time she was the most beautiful girl I'd ever seen.

Psychiatrist: Did she have a large bosom?

Harold: I don't know – I never saw them.

Psychiatrist: Never?

Harold: No. (*Psychiatrist reacts*) They felt average.

Psychiatrist: Average?

Harold: If that's any help.

Psychiatrist: (*disappointed*) I see. Carry on.

Harold: She was the poshest bird I'd ever met. Such breeding. She was the first girl I'd known who ate her peas with the back of her fork. Very impressed with that, I was. She was rich as well, loaded her family were, and there was only her and her old lady. The old man was dead, I could have had the lot – fourteen breweries. Anyway, I couldn't put it off any longer, her mother insisted on coming round to meet my family – *him*. So I arranged for them to call on us for tea. I got home early that afternoon, got washed and dressed and went downstairs to the lounge.

SCENE 8

The lounge. Harold enters. Albert is sitting in front of the electric fire with his socks on, warming his feet. Steam is rising from them. Harold's trousers have the creases down the sides.

Harold: Did you finish them?

Albert: Yeah.

Harold: You bloody idiot! Look what you've done to my trousers.

Albert: What's wrong with them?

Harold: You've put the creases down the sides. That's my best suit. It's my only suit. And take those rotten socks off, you smell like a team of Turkish wrestlers.

Albert: I've just washed these, I'm drying them.

Harold: Why don't you take them off when you wash them? *(He opens the wardrobe and throws the old man a pair of socks)* Here you are, wear mine. And hurry up and get ready, they'll be here in a minute. *(He is changing his trousers)*

Albert: I am ready. I've only got to put my boots on.

Harold: You're not going to meet them dressed like that?

Albert: It's my house, they'll take me as they find me.

Harold: I know where the police'll find you. Dad, you know tonight is important for me, you could have made the effort for once, just once. Have you had a bath?

Albert: Yes.

Harold: I mean recently. Within the last six months?

Albert: I don't have baths in the winter, you know that.

Harold: You don't have too many in the summer either.

Albert: What's the point? You only get dirty again.

Harold: What about your hands – come on – hands. They'll expect to shake hands with you.

Albert: The way you've been going on about them I thought I'd have to curtsey.

Harold: Are you going to wash your hands?

Albert: No. I'll keep my mittens on.

Harold: You're doing it on purpose, aren't you? You're deliberately trying to coal-box it.

Albert: I can't understand why you're going to all this trouble.

Harold: Because I'm trying to make a good impression, aren't I? Her mother doesn't like me. She doesn't want to see her daughter get tied up with the likes of me.

Albert: You can't blame her.

Harold: I don't blame her.

Albert: Then why did you invite her round?

Harold: I had to, I had no choice. I was pushed into a corner. Before giving her consent to the marriage she insisted on meeting the bloodstock. You. Oh gawd, why didn't I tell her you were dead like I usually do?

Albert: All right, then. If it's so important to you, when she gets here I'll turn on the old charm. I'll have her eating out of my hand.

Harold: No, don't – she'll go down with bubonic plague. Have you got the tea ready?

Albert: Yes.

Harold: Did you make the cucumber sandwiches?

Albert: Under the cloth.

(Harold takes a cloth off a plate, revealing a French loaf cut up into nine-inch sections with half a cucumber, cut lengthways, inside each sandwich. Harold picks one up and opens it. He takes the cucumber out.)

Harold: You don't cut them in half. You slice them delicately. On little bits of bread. Little thin ones, that size *(draws a tiny square in the air)*.

Albert: They're no good, one burp and you're empty.

Harold: She won't be able to get her choppers through them. She's not a French lorry-driver. Oh gawd, what a disaster this is going to be.

(There is a knock at the front door)

Harold: They're here! Dad, please. Do your best. Don't let me down. I'll introduce you, you shake hands and go to bed, all right? *(He picks up an aerosol, sprays it in the air, then sprays it over the old man. He turns Albert round and sprays down his back)*

Albert: Get off. Leave me alone.

Harold: And no dirty jokes. Best behaviour. No effing and blinding, and don't get too near them. *(He goes into the hallway)*

(Albert picks up the cucumber, takes a bite out of it then puts the rest back between the two slices of bread. He scratches his head, picks something out of his hair, looks at it between finger and thumb. He shrugs and flicks it away. His head describes a series of arcs as he watches the thing jump away.

Harold re-enters followed by Mrs Kennington-Stroud and her daughter, Bunty. Both are dressed in mink coats)

Harold: Do come in.

(Mrs Kennington-Stroud looks round the room with an expression of distaste)

Bunty: Oh Mummy, isn't it absolutely super?

Mrs Stroud: *(sourly)* Delightful. *(She gathers her coat tightly round her)*

Bunty: *(trying to jolly things along)* Darling, how on earth did you find a place like this?

Harold: It wasn't easy. *(Pause)* We were looking for years, and then one day Harrods phoned me up and we bought it on the spot. Permit me to introduce my father. This is Bunty, my intended.

Albert: Hello, luv. Nice to meet you.

Bunty: Hello. Darling, he's nice. He doesn't seem anything like a misery-guts.

Harold: And this, pater, is Bunty's mater.

Albert: *(taking her hand)* Charmed, I'm sure. It's a great pleasure to make your acquaintance, madam. *(He kisses her hand)*

Harold: *(wincing)* Well, I expect you'll be wanting to go to bed now, Father.

Mrs Stroud: Just one moment. Am I to take it you actually live here?

Albert: Yeah. All my life.

Mrs Stroud: It seems that I have been somewhat misled. I understood your son to tell me that you were a race-horse owner and lived next to the stables near Ascot.

Albert: No, missis, he meant Acton. Well, it's more Shepherd's Bush, really. I expect you're like me, a bit Mutt and Jeff.

Mrs Stroud: I beg your pardon?

Albert: *(louder)* Cook and chef. *(Taps his ear)* Deaf.

Harold: Don't shout, Father. I assure you I had no intention of deliberately misleading you, Mrs Kennington-Stroud. We do in fact own a horse and . . . may I divest you of your outer garment?

Mrs Stroud: *(clutching her coat even tighter)* No, thank you, I have no intention of staying.

Bunty: Oh, don't be such a bore, Mother, we've only just arrived.

Albert: Perhaps the old biddy's a bit parky – shall I put another bar on?

Harold: Perhaps I may proffer you a little sherry, to mitigate the ardour of the vexing journey you entailed getting here?

Mrs Stroud: *(puzzled)* Are you English, Mr Steptoe?

Harold: I beg your pardon?

Bunty: Mother, please. Yes, darling, we would love some sherry.

Harold: Oh, that's good. Because I have recently of late been fortunate enough to procure from my purveyor . . . a beautifully modulated Olarosa selected from a Salero from the finest bodiga in Jerez . . .

Mrs Stroud: Young man, if you mean you've got some sherry, then say so, simply.

Harold: Yes, I have half a bottle. Father, the sherry glasses. *(He goes and gets the bottle. Albert gets four specimen glasses)*

Mrs Stroud: What are *they*?

Albert: They were a job lot from the local hospital.

Mrs Stroud: They are specimen glasses!

Albert: There's nothing wrong with them, I washed them out.

Harold: *(rushing over and snatching them from Albert)* Not them. I told you never to use them in company. I do beg your pardon, we do have some apposite drinking vessels. We keep them for best.

Mrs Stroud: I don't think we'll bother. I think it's time we were leaving.

Harold: No, no, don't go. You haven't had your tea. I've got it all ready – voilà. A cold collation. Cucumber sandwiches, fairy cakes, fresh cream sandwich.

Albert: A tin of biscuits.

Harold: Shut up. Please sit down. Father, show Mrs Stroud a chair.

Albert: Over there. That's a chair.

Harold: Convey her to it, pater.

Albert: *(posh)* Oh, I do beg your pardon. *(He offers her his crooked elbow)* May I escort you to your chair? *(He leads her over to the upholstered chair)* Allow me. Park your bum on that. *(He bangs the chair with his hand. Dust rises. He sits her down and picks up the plate of cucumber sandwiches)* Cucumber sandwich?

(Mrs Stroud takes one of the huge sandwiches and holds it)

Harold: *(to Bunty)* It's all going wrong.

Bunty: Don't worry, just be yourself and stop acting. She likes you.

(Harold pours the tea out from a teapot with a tea cosy on it. He carries the tray over to Mrs Stroud)

Harold: The milk's already in. But it's Old Grey.

(Mrs Stroud takes a cup. Albert picks up the sugar bowl)

Albert: Sugar?

Mrs Stroud: Thank you.

Albert: How many lumps?

Mrs Stroud: Two.

Albert: Hey, you dropped your sandwiches, missus. *(He picks up two lumps in his fingers and drops them in her cup)*

(Harold gives Bunty a cup and takes one himself. He sits down. They are now all sitting down. They sip their tea)

Harold: Well, this is nice.

(Albert dunks a biscuit in his tea. He eats half of it, then dunks the last bit. It falls in. He fishes for it with his spoon. Harold reacts with disgust. Mrs Stroud winces, her back straightens. Albert slurps his tea)

Harold: Sunningdale must be looking rather lovely at this time of the year.

Mrs Stroud: *(scratching herself surreptitiously)* Yes.

Harold: You really ought to see their house, Father. The rhododendrons are quite splendid.

> *(Albert slurps his tea again. Mrs Stroud scratches herself a bit harder somewhere else. She is looking worried)*

Harold: How many gardeners do you have, Bunty?

Bunty: Oh, I don't know, seven or eight.

Harold: Imagine that, Father – seven gardeners.

> *(Albert pours his tea into the saucer and sips it. Mrs Stroud is now scratching herself more vigorously)*

Harold: The house is quite delightful too. Tudor, isn't it?

> *(Bunty starts scratching herself. Harold is looking a bit worried. He looks at Bunty and her mother. Mrs Stroud is now scratching herself all over. Bunty scratches a bit harder as well)*

Mrs Stroud: Something peculiar is happening. *(She scratches again, then screams)*

Albert: *(dropping his cup and saucer)* What's the matter with you?

Mrs Stroud: Something just leapt on to the table.

Harold: Where, where?

Mrs Stroud: There. *(Screams)* There's another one.

> *(Harold and Albert look for it. Bunty screams)*

Bunty: *(brushing herself feverishly)* There – on the table.

Mrs Stroud: A microscopic animal.

Harold: Oh no – not fleas.

> *(Both the women jump and start feverishly brushing themselves down. They take their coats off and shake them)*

Harold: It's all right, it's nothing to worry about. They're probably off the horse, I shouldn't think for a moment they're human fleas. *(To Albert)* I'll kill you.

Mrs Stroud: How could you bring me to a house with fleas?

Albert: If there's any fleas in this house, missus, you brought them in.

Mrs Stroud: How dare you! *(She screams and scratches herself frantically)*

Harold: Don't panic, it'll be all right, I've got some DDT. *(He picks up a canister of DDT and squirts it over her. She screams and rushes out of the room)* Mrs Stroud, come back! *(He goes to the door. Bunty goes with him. He turns to her)* Bunty, please, I . . . hang on. *(He slaps her sharply on the back of her head)*

Bunty: How dare you! *(She smacks him round the face)* I must have been mad. *(She goes out)*

Harold: No, Bunty, I wasn't walloping you, I was – Bunty, does this mean it's all off?

(The front door slams. Harold turns back into the room. He stares hatefully at the old man)

Albert: You know what I reckon? I reckon it was that mattress I bought yesterday. I didn't like the look of the bloke, I thought he looked a bit cooty.

Harold: You know what I'm going to do with you? I'm going to take you out into the yard, I'm going to take all your clothes off, I'm going to turn the hosepipe on and I'm going to . . . *(He suddenly scratches himself furiously)* You've given them to me now. *(He shivers in revulsion)* Ugh, Ugh. *(He rushes out of the room)*

Albert: That's funny, they don't bother me.

SCENE 9
The psychiatrist's consulting room. Harold is lying on the couch. The psychiatrist is still doodling.

Harold: I was covered in them. I had to have all my hair shaved off and I never went out of the house for a month. Bald as a coot, I was.

Psychiatrist: *(inadvertently scratching himself)* Yes, yes, most distressing.

Harold: Now I come to think of it, it's a wonder I haven't tried to kill him before. What do you think, doctor? Am I going off my chump?

Psychiatrist: Good Lord, no. There's nothing to worry about. It's a classical case of a subconscious wish fulfilment. These things are quite a common result of the hypertension that exists when two people live in such close proximity in claustrophobic surroundings, unable to pursue their outside interests. It happens all the time with married couples. I'll give you some tranquillizers and what I suggest you do is this . . .

SCENE 10
The lounge. Albert is sitting at the table writing out a large notice. It reads 'Room to let £5 per week'. Harold comes in. Albert yells in fear and runs round the other side of the table.

Albert: Keep away from me! Don't you touch me – they'll soon find out you've escaped. The van'll be here in a minute.

Harold: What are you talking about?

Albert: Didn't they put you away?

Harold: Of course they didn't. There's nothing wrong with me.

Albert: Nothing wrong with you? Trying to kill your own father?

Harold: I've had it all explained to me. I've had a long chat with the psychiatrist. He explained the cause of my temporary aberration, and now I understand the reasons and philosophically accept them, he assures me it won't happen again. From now on I shall be a different person. With the help of my tranquillizers. *(Rattles a bottle)* What are you doing there?

Albert: Nothing.

Harold: Don't be frightened. I won't hurt you. *(He looks at the notice)* Room to let. Whose room?

Albert: Yours.

Harold: Mine?

Albert: I took it for granted they'd bung you straight in the nut-house. Well, I've got to have some source of income, haven't I . . .

Harold: You callous little – I've been out of the house three hours and you want to let my room. I've never – no. No. I'm not going to let you get on top of me again. I can see your point of view – old man – no income. Yes. Very reasonable. *(He takes a tranquillizer)* No, it's all changed. There's nothing you can ever do that will upset me. *(He goes to the wardrobe, takes out his tennis rackets, and puts his whites into a holdall with Dunlop written on the side)*

Albert: Where are you going?

Harold: I am going to pursue my outside interests. I am going down to the tennis club. There's a very lovely girl gets down there on Thursdays, I think she fancies me. She's an extremely good player and with a bit of luck I might be able to get a game with her.

Albert: What's her name?

Harold: Christine.

Albert: Not the blonde with the big bristols?

Harold: *(suspiciously)* Yes.

Albert: You're too late, mate, I'm playing her at half past four.

Harold: I beg your pardon?

Albert: Yeah. I joined this morning. Smashing club, ain't it? Lend us one of your rackets – mine is going home a bit.

(Harold tries to control himself, his face working. He swallows another pill. He can't control his twitching face. He picks up the

carving knife. His arm is shaking. He grabs hold of it with his other hand to stop himself from raising the knife above his head. Finally he can't control himself. He roars with anger and lunges at the old man. Albert screams and runs round the room with Harold after him. Albert runs out of the door, followed by Harold)

Harold: I'll kill you – I'll murder you! I don't care what happens to me.

Divided We Stand

First transmission 28 March 1972

Divided We Stand was produced by David Croft

SCENE 1
The Steptoes' lounge. Harold and Albert are surrounded by wall-paper pattern books, paint colour charts, carpet pattern books, curtain material samples, etc. They are going through the wall-paper books.

Harold: *(exasperated)* We've been going through these books for three weeks now and we haven't agreed on one bleeding room. Well, at least can we try and agree on the colour scheme of the bog?

Albert: I just don't like anything you've suggested. I'm entitled to my opinion.

Harold: No, you're not. You've got no taste. You never have had. Decorating a house out is a skilled job. Everything has to harmonize and blend. You can't just bung anything up on the walls.

Albert: I like it the way it is.

Harold: Well, I don't. When was this place last decorated?

Albert: After the war.

Harold: Exactly – 1918. It hasn't had a lick of paint on it since then, nothing.

Albert: It don't need it. That wallpaper's as good as the day your mother put it up.

Harold: It's filthy. It's dark. It's depressing. A house like this should be light and gay.

Albert: I like chocolate paint. Dark green and chocolate. They're the colours. Last for years. Never shows the dirt.

Harold: Well, paint yourself in it then. We're not having it in here. Look, Dad, use your imagination. Let me explain it again and try to visualize it. *(Harold takes the paint chart)* Look. Wedgwood blue on the ceiling . . .

Albert: Ugh.

Harold: I haven't finished. (*Takes another chart*) Etruscan red for the woodwork . . . then . . . (*opens a wallpaper book*) this wallpaper . . . and . . . (*picks up a carpet pattern book*) this carpet on the floor. How's that?

Albert: Bleeding awful. It'll look like a Peruvian brothel.
    (*Harold throws the pattern book down in disgust*)

Harold: Oh, I give up. What chance have you got? (*Holds up a magazine*) Look, *House and Garden* – the self-same colour scheme. Same wallpaper, same carpet. It's delightful.

Albert: That's Blenheim Palace.

Harold: It doesn't make any difference. It'll work just as well in here. You must be bold, Dad. You mustn't be frightened. You mustn't be afraid of experiment.

Albert: Hmm. How much is that paper?

Harold: (*looks on the back of the pattern*) Nine pounds a roll.

Albert: Nine pounds? Your mother did this whole place out for that.

Harold: Father, things have gone up a bit since then.

Albert: Well, that's not going up, I'm telling you. What a waste of money. We've got five hundred gallons of ex-Army camouflage paint outside, why can't we bung that up? We could do the outside as well.

Harold: Well, yes, yes, if you're expecting to be dive-bombed at any minute, I can see the point. But this happens to be a house, not a tank factory. Look, if we don't hurry up and choose something, next year's patterns will be out.

Albert: How many books have you got there?

Harold: Seven.

Albert: Well, there you are, bung them all up. I'll sew all these carpet patterns together, it won't cost us a penny.

Harold: (*rising*) You would, wouldn't you?

Albert: Certainly. I don't mind it looking rotten if it don't cost anything. It's when it costs a fortune and looks rotten I object to.

Harold: It won't look rotten.

Albert: (*flicking through a pattern book*) I like this hairy paper.

Harold: That's not hairy paper, it's flock.

Albert: It's nice, ain't it?

Harold: It's quite elegant. Albeit a trifle ostentatious. Where were you visualizing putting it?

Albert: In the khazi.

Harold: We're not putting flock wallpaper in the khazi. We're having something washable out there.

Albert: It's not me who writes on the wall.

Harold: It is you. It's when you're sitting out there doing your crosswords. Covered in anagrams, it is. And worse. Some of the graffiti is disgusting. It's positively Pompeian.

Albert: That ain't me – I can't reach that high. That's the customers do that. You shouldn't let them use it. Staff only, that should be.

Harold: We're still not having flock wallpaper in the khazi.

Albert: And we're not having Wedgwood blue on the ceiling in here. (*He sits*)

Harold: I see. And that is your final word?

Albert: Yes.

Harold: So it would appear we have reached an impasse?

Albert: If you like.

Harold: You won't give way on anything, will you? You don't give a monkey's what colour we have. You just want to go against me. If I wanted flock wallpaper in the bog, you wouldn't. Whatever I want, you don't.

Albert: I'm entitled to my opinion.

Harold: (*rising and walking up and down*) It's not just the decorations. It's everything. Every idea I have about improvements . . . improving the business, improving the house, anything – you're against it. You frustrate everything I've ever wanted to do. You're a dyed-in-the-wool Fascist reactionary squalid little know-your-place don't-rise-above-yourself don't-move-out-of-your-hole complacent little turd.

Albert: Who do you think . . .

Harold: I haven't finished yet. You're mentally, physically, spiritually a festering fly-blown heap of accumulated filth.

Albert: What do you want for your tea?

Harold: I don't want any tea. You're going to hear me out. You enjoy living in squalor, don't you?

Albert: No, I don't.

Harold: You do. Look at it! When did you last clean this room out?

Albert: Yesterday.

Harold: Liar! (*Runs his hand along the top of his desk*) Look at that.

Albert: It's only dust.

Harold: Dust? That's not dust, that's top soil. If you leave it much longer we won't need a vacuum cleaner, we'll need a bleeding plough . . . (*Next to the goldfish bowl is a mug in a saucer*) And this

. . . (He picks up the mug, the saucer comes up with it, stuck together. Harold prises the mug off the saucer and shoves it in Albert's face) What's that in there?

Albert: That's coffee dregs.

Harold: Coffee dregs? It's got more hairs on it than that flock wallpaper. That's pure penicillin, that is. And what about this lot? *(He goes over to a great pile of newspapers in the corner. He pulls some out from near the top. A cloud of dust flies out. He reads a headline)* 'Mr Chamberlain returns from meeting with Herr Hitler' *(Throws the paper down, reads the next one)* 'Fort Belvedere, Friday. "I'm giving up my throne for the woman I love."' *(Throws it away. Reads next one)* 'Wellington Koo meets President Roosevelt.' *(Throws it away. Reads next one)* 'Princess Margaret joins Brownies.'

(Albert has got interested and picks up a paper)

Albert: I remember this: 'Mussolini invades Albania. King Zog flees.'

Harold: That's nothing, mate, we've got king size fleas in here. It's disgusting. This house is like a pigsty. Filth, filth, filth. And it smells as well.

Albert: I can't smell anything.

Harold: Of course you can't. You smell worse than the house does. Every day I come in here, I open the door and there it is. You smell like a pair of zoo-keeper's boots. I've had enough. The place should be cleaned out every day. *(He starts moving objects around the room. Behind every item of furniture there are various bits of junk)* None of this has been moved in years. Ration books – gas masks – a packet of dried eggs – and . . . what's these? *(He picks up a pair of false teeth)*

Albert: Let me have a look. *(Takes the teeth)* Gorblimey, I wondered where they'd got to. They're my old teeth. I lost them in 1941. They flew out when that land mine dropped down the road. Well, well, well, that's a bit of luck, they're the best teeth I ever had. Ooh, that's lovely. They don't make teeth like them these days. *(He ducks to put them in)* Oh gawd, me gums have shrunk. *(He changes his teeth)*

Harold: That is the most revolting thing I've ever seen in my life. That's it, I'm finished. I refuse to live in this filth any longer. I shall be perfectly frank. Unless something is done about it, I shall be forced to make alternative arrangements.

Albert: Do what you like.

Harold: The pattern of our lives has grown too diverse for any chance of reconciliation.

Albert: If you like.

Harold: Your mere presence tends to impinge upon my aesthetic pleasures and moments of relaxation.

Albert: In other words I get on your tits.

Harold: Crude, but apposite. The only possible course of action left open is for one of us to go. Agreed?

Albert: Agreed.

Harold: Right.

Albert: Right.

Harold: No hard feelings?

Albert: No. I'll be glad to get rid of you.

Harold: What do you mean? I'm not going!

Albert: Well, I'm not going.

Harold: I can't go. I can't afford to go.

Albert: Then you'll have to stay here, won't you? You'll have to put up with it.

Harold: No. I'm not going to put up with it. I want to live on my own. I want some privacy. And I'm going to have it. (*He goes to the door*)

Albert: Oh yeah. How?

Harold: Well, if you won't move, there's only one thing we can do.

Albert: What's that?

Harold: Apartheid, mate. Separate development. (*He leaves the room*)

Albert: (*puzzled*) Apartheid? What the bleeding hell's apartheid?

SCENE 2

The lounge has been partitioned in half. The partitioning starts in the doorway, dividing the door frame in half. It divides the table in two and runs up to the television set in the foreground. It is obvious that a further piece is to be added thereby dividing the television set in two. In the left-hand half (Harold's half) of the room, Harold is nailing battening on to a piece of hardboard which is cut to fit the television set. It is obviously the missing part of the partition. A sawing trestle, odd bits of hardboard and battening lie around. Albert walks in and watches Harold, a look of scorn on his face.

Albert: Bloody silly idea.

Harold: If you don't like it you know what you can do.

Albert: You're just bringing the value of the property down.

Harold: Not as far as I'm concerned. I should have done this years ago, it would have saved me a lot of aggravation. Would you mind, please? *(He pushes the old man to one side and fits the bit of partitioning which he has been making over the television set. He stands back and admires it)* There. Partition is complete. The border has been sealed.

Albert: It's a wonder you haven't got any armed guards walking along the top of it, a couple of searchlights at each end.

Harold: What are you doing here? I don't recall inviting you into my home. You are persona non grata as far as I'm concerned. I would appreciate it if you would retire to your own rat-hole.

Albert: This is it, then, is it? You're not taking it up to the ceiling?

Harold: Unfortunately it's not practical, seeing as how the only window is on your side. However, I shall be having the upper part of the partition double glazed, thus letting the light in and keeping you out. Well, there it is, two self-contained flats. Complete privacy for both of us – except, of course, in no-man's land.

Albert: Where's that?

Harold: Out here. *(He leads the way out into the hall. The old man follows him)*

SCENE 3

The hall. This has been partitioned with hardboard straight down the middle. The hardboard is around five feet six high, the main framing going up to the 'ceiling'. The hardboard continues along the hallway up to a yard from the lounge door. This gap is filled with a turnstile. We can see up the stairs and these have also been partitioned with hardboard straight up the middle.

Harold: Voilà. Checkpoint Charlie. Not entirely satisfactory, but it's the only way I could think of giving me access to the stairs and you access to the kitchen. I think that's all. Outside of business hours, I see no reason why our paths should ever cross again.

Albert: Suits me.

Harold: And now, if you wouldn't mind retiring to your own quarters, I wish to be alone.

(He pushes the old man through a swing gate in the partition by the

turnstile, swings it back into position and padlocks it. Albert is now on the upstage side of the turnstile in his own half of the hall and Harold is on the down-stage side of the turnstile in his half. Albert tries the turnstile and finds that it is locked)

Albert: It's locked.

Harold: You have to put a penny in it.

Albert: I'm not paying a penny every time I want to go to the kitchen.

Harold: I shall have to pay a penny every time I want to go to bed. We'll have a share-out at the end of the year.

Albert: That's not fair. I'll want to go to the kitchen more times a day than you'll want to go to bed. Three meals a day, cups of tea, washing up. It's going to cost me twopence a time. Penny to get in, penny to get out. It's going to cost me a fortune. Why can't you put one of them non-paying ones in?

Harold: Because that's the only one we've got.

Albert: *(rattling the turnstile)* That's mine anyway. I got that when they knocked the ladies' bog down at the dog track.

Harold: It's not yours, that is an asset of the business. Look, I'll tell you what we'll do, we'll put a blackboard up and every time we go through we'll mark it up with a piece of chalk, then at the end of the year we'll open it up and share it out pro rata. It'll be better than the Christmas club down at the Skinners Arms. You always have that out by Easter.

Albert: I don't trust you. You'll rub mine off.

Harold: I won't rub yours off.

Albert: Well, you'll add some to your score.

Harold: What a petty little criminal mind you've got. I'm not interested in nicking paltry sums of money off of you. You can have the lot if you like, I'm just trying to get rid of you. Now will you please go home, it's getting late. Go on.

(Albert takes out a penny and puts it in the turnstile. He goes through)

Albert: I want a drink of water. That's one to me.

Harold: Yes. Goodnight.

(Albert goes into the kitchen. Harold goes into his half of the lounge)

SCENE 4
The lounge.

Harold: Free! On my own at last. Privacy for the first time in my life. Peace, quiet.

(*Door bangs. Harold then sees over the top of the partition the old man's hat coming in his door. The hat moves along the partition. Then we see more and more of Albert appear over the top of the partition as he walks up a ramp. Albert leans on the top of the partition looking into Harold's half of the room*)

Albert: Harold, I'm lonely. Can I come in for a game of cards?

Harold: No, you can't. And put that ramp back in the yard. I will not have you looking over the wall like bleeding Chad. Get down. I'm going to put *frosted* glass up there. Go on, get down.

(*Albert turns and walks back down the ramp so that now only his hat can be seen*)

Harold: And take your hat off.

(*Albert's hat disappears. Now we can't see anything of him. Silence for a little while. Harold relents*)

Harold: Goodnight.

(*There is a loud raspberry from the other side of the partition*)

SCENE 5
The yard. It is the next day. The front door of the house has now been removed and in its place are two separate narrow doors each with its own keyhole, door knocker and letter box. The old man's door is on the left and has number 24 on it. It is a traditional brown-panelled wooden door. Harold's door is painted a trendy yellow, with an opaque fluted glass centre panel with wrought iron scrollwork on the outside of the glass. It is numbered 24a. By the side of Harold's door is a small bay tree in a tub. Harold and Albert come out of their respective doors in their dressing-gowns.

Harold: Good morning.

Albert: Good morning.

Harold: Lovely morning.

Albert: Very nice.

(*Harold picks up a small watering can and waters his bay tree. They both pick up their milk and go back inside*)

SCENE 6

The hall. Albert and Harold walk along their respective halves of the hall. They pass either side of the turnstile. The door to the lounge has also been divided into two narrow doors. They open their respective doors, go inside the lounge and close the doors. A pause.

Harold comes out of his lounge door, puts a penny in the turnstile, goes through it. There is a blackboard nailed to the wall. It is divided in half, one side marked 'Harold', the other 'Dad'. Each half has several chalk marks on it, Dad's half more than Harold's. Harold chalks another mark against his name and goes up his half of the stairs.

Albert comes out of his door, puts a penny in the turnstile, chalks a mark against his name, looks round and slyly chalks up another mark for himself. He goes through the turnstile and walks off to the kitchen.

Harold comes back down the stairs to the turnstile. He puts a penny in and goes through. He chalks up a mark against his name, looks at Albert's side of the blackboard, reacts to it with resignation, and wipes off Albert's last chalkmark. He walks off to the kitchen.

SCENE 7

The kitchen. This room has also been divided down the middle. At one end the partition divides the sink and the window. The gas stove has been moved to the centre of the kitchen so that it is now a free-standing cooker. The partition divides it in half.

Albert is standing by his half of the gas stove. Harold enters and goes up to his half of the gas stove. He strikes a match.

Harold: *(calls)* Top left. *(He lights the top left burner)*
Albert: *(calls)* Bottom right.
　　(Harold turns a gas tap. On his side of the divided stove, Albert lights the bottom right hand burner. They pick up their kettles and go over to the sink. There is a swivel mixer tap. In the partition is a slot the same shape as the mixer tap. The tap is on Harold's side. Harold turns it on and starts to fill his kettle. There is a piece of string down from the slot. Albert pulls it and the mixer tap comes through the slot from Harold's side with the string attached to it)
Harold: Do you mind, I'm filling my kettle. *(He pulls his bit of string and the mixer tap comes back through the slot onto his side)*

Albert: Oi, what's your bleeding game? (*He pulls his string and the tap comes back through the slot*)

(*A tug of war develops, each pulling on his own bit of string, so the tap slides backwards and forwards through the slot, still running. Finally, when the mixer tap is on his side, Harold picks up a pair of scissors and cuts Albert's string*)

Albert: (*holding a loose piece of string*) You bastard!

(*Harold laughs and continues filling his kettle*)

SCENE 8

The lounge. It is evening. Each half of the room is dressed with their respective belongings. Harold is seated at his half of the dinner table, dressed in a smoking jacket, eating out of tins. Albert is seated on the other side of the partition at his half of the table, tucking into a large meal. Frosted glass panels have been added to the top of the partition, so the separation is now complete.

Harold sprinkles salt and pepper on his dinner from silver cruets. He puts them down. A small hatchway slides open in the partition and Albert's hand comes through and takes the cruets. The hatchway slides shut.

Harold opens hatch and peers through.

Harold: Give me my cruets back.

Albert: They're not your cruets.

Harold: They are. I bought them myself. They're solid silver.

Albert: I gave you half the money.

Harold: You lent me half the money.

Albert: And till I get it back they're just as much mine as yours. A joint possession is a joint possession. You can have the salt. (*His hand comes through the hatchway and puts the salt cellar back. He shuts panel*)

Harold: (*opening panel*) That's no good, they're a pair. You can't split up a pair. You ought to know that.

Albert: You've split us up.

Harold: That's different. You're not Georgian. Or valuable. Give me my pepper pot.

Albert: You can have this one.

(*Albert's hand comes through the hatchway with the funniest-looking child's pepper pot it is possible to find. He puts it down and shuts panel*)

Harold: Thank you very much. That's ideal, that is. A perfect match with my King's pattern knife and fork.

Albert: Give us seventy-five quid and you can have the other one back. (*He shuts the hatchway*)

Harold: I haven't got seventy-five quid, have I? I spent it all on the partition. And you keep your hands on your side. As soon as I can afford my own stuff I'm nailing that up.

Albert: I can't hear a word you're saying.

Harold: (*opening shutter*) I said as soon as I can afford my – oh go away.

(*Harold slams the hatchway shut. He gets up and starts setting up for a night's television viewing. He moves his chair into position, sits down, picks up the* Radio Times, *chooses a programme. He leans forward to switch on and only then realizes all the knobs are on the old man's side. Harold goes over to the hatchway on the partition. The hatchway slides open. Albert peers through*)

Albert: Who is it?

Harold: Next door. Would you mind switching the television set on?

Albert: What programme?

Harold: BBC2.

Albert: Hang on.

(*The hatchway slides shut. Albert looks at the TV programmes in the newspaper*)

Albert: Royal Festival Hall. Margot Fonteyn and Rudolph Nureyev. *Les Sylphides* – dirty devils. (*He switches the set on*)

(*Harold settles back in his chair, watching his half of the screen*)

Harold: I hope they don't dance too far apart.

(*The set comes on. Ballet. Harold starts humming the music, leaning on one side in the hope of seeing more of the screen. Albert looks fed up. He reacts in disgust*)

Albert: (*calling*) Harold, you want to come round this side, her drawers have just fallen down.

Harold: Liar!

Albert: (*cackles and watches for a few more seconds*) Oh gawd, I can't watch this all night. (*Picks up the TV programmes*) ITV – *Blood of The Ripper*. Ah, that's more like it.

(*Harold is enjoying the ballet. Suddenly the picture changes to a close-up of a ghoul screaming. Harold gets up and goes over to the partition. He knocks on the hatchway. The hatchway slides open. Albert peers through*)

Albert: What do you want now? I'm trying to watch the television.

Harold: That is not BBC2.

Albert: I know it's not.

Harold: I specifically want to watch Rudolph Nureyev and Margaret Fontana.

Albert: I'm not watching that rubbish.

Harold: We agreed that Mondays, Wednesdays and Fridays should be my choice of programmes, and Tuesdays, Thursdays and Saturdays your choice, with us each having every alternate Sunday.

Albert: That's right.

Harold: Today is Wednesday. I want BBC2 on.

Albert: Well, I don't.

Harold: That is a very unfair attitude to adopt. We made an agreement. We shook hands on it. I've got the law of contract on my side.

Albert: I've got the knobs on my side. (*Harold reaches through the hatchway and grabs Albert by the scruff of the neck and pulls his head through the partition. Albert yells*) Oh, let go, you're hurting me.

Harold: Are you going to put BBC2 on?

Albert: No. (*Harold squeezes. Albert yells*) You're strangling me.

Harold: Put the ballet back on.

Albert: All right, all right, let go. (*Harold lets go. Albert rubs his neck*) I'm not putting the ballet on.

Harold: You wait till you come out of there, I'll murder you.

 (*Albert is worried about this*)

Albert: (*wheedling*) I don't want to watch the ballet, Harold, it drives me round the twist. I'll tell you what, let's compromise. We'll watch BBC1 tonight, then you can have another turn tomorrow.

Harold: What's on BBC1?

Albert: Football. European Cup.

Harold: Hmm. That's not bad. All right then, we'll watch BBC1.

 (*Albert goes over and turns on BBC1. A football match is on. He sits down. Harold is also sitting down watching. He gets interested. He follows the path of the ball as it goes over to Albert's side of the screen*)

Harold: (*calling*) Was that a goal?

Albert: No, he saved it.

Harold: Oh, gawd. (*He is now getting very interested in the game, urging the players on, calling out 'Man on', 'Turn', 'Man up your back'. Suddenly the set starts moving into Albert's side of the room.*

There are only a few inches left on Harold's side when he jumps up and grabs it. He pulls it back) Leave it alone!

Albert: You've got more screen than I have.

Harold: *(pulling)* I haven't. It's split right down the middle. Let go.

Albert: It's a twenty-one inch screen and I'm entitled to ten and a half inches.

Harold: You've got ten and a half inches.

Albert: I haven't. I've only got nine inches. Let go.

Harold: Oh, all right then, have the bleeding lot.

(Harold lets go. Albert falls. Harold is gleeful. Albert settles down to watch. Harold gets an evil thought. He picks up flex and moves to wall. Albert is enjoying himself. Harold pulls out plug)

Harold: *(laughs)* Normal service will be resumed tomorrow. In the meantime we are going to bed. From all of us here at the three pin plug, goodnight, everybody, goodnight. *(Sings the first three bars of the National Anthem. He yawns and looks at his watch, then goes over to the door, switches his light out and goes into the hallway)*

SCENE 9

The hall. Albert comes out of his side of the lounge at the same time. They look at each other across the turnstile, then they both run to their front doors.

SCENE 10

The yard. Albert and Harold come out of their front doors and race each other over to the outside toilet. Albert gets there first and opens the door. They run in.

The outside toilet has also been divided by partition. The lavatory pan has been boxed in with a door on either side to give them both access to it from their respective halves. Harold rushes over and opens his door only to find the old man has got there first.

Harold: Come on out of there, you don't want to go.

Albert: Yes, I do.

Harold: You don't. You only want to go because I want to go.

Albert: I was here first. You'll have to wait.

(Harold is frustrated. He slams his door shut. He is fuming. He suddenly has an idea. He reaches over the top of the partition and pulls the chain. The toilet flushes . . . Albert yells)

Albert: You rotten little toe-rag.
   (*Harold laughs. He goes out of the toilet and crosses the yard into the house*)

SCENE 11
The kitchen. There is a saucepan of milk boiling on the gas stove. It starts to boil over. Harold quickly whips the saucepan off the gas. He pours the milk into a mug. He goes out of the kitchen, switching the light off.

SCENE 12
The hall. Harold puts a penny in the turnstile, goes through and chalks a mark against his name on the blackboard. Albert comes in and they meet at the foot of the stairs. Albert glares at Harold.

Harold: Goodnight, Father.
Albert: Cobblers.
Harold: And the same to you.
Albert: Cobblers.
Harold: They make a fine big stew.

SCENE 13
The kitchen. It is dark. The gas ring is still alight and burning fiercely. There is a tea towel hanging from a hook on the partition over the gas rings on Harold's side. The towel starts smouldering.

SCENE 14
Film clip of fire engine with bell clanging, tearing down a street.

SCENE 15
A hospital ward. Harold and Albert are lying in adjacent beds, coughing. There are oxygen cylinders by their bedsides.

Albert: Oh gawd, I'm dying. It's your fault. If you hadn't put them bloody silly partitions up, this wouldn't have happened. The bleeding firemen had to put pennies in the turnstiles to get at us.

Harold: *(patiently)* That was because they came in the wrong door. If they'd come in your door they wouldn't have had any trouble at all.

Albert: Oh, they know that, don't they? They're always going to houses with turnstiles in the passageway. They're used to it. Just because you wanted to be on your own. Because you wanted to get away from me. Well, look where it's got us.

Harold: *(sadly)* Yeah, and in the same ward.

Albert: Yeah, well, you'll have to put up with it. Here, give us some of your orange juice. They ain't given me any. Come on, hurry up, I'm thirsty.

(Harold patiently picks up the jug of orange juice on his bedside table . . . and throws the lot over the old man. Albert yells)

The Desperate Hours

First transmission 3 April 1972

The Desperate Hours featured
Leonard Rossiter as Spooner
with
J. G. Devlin as Ferris
and was produced by John Howard Davies

SCENE 1
The Steptoes' lounge. Harold and Albert are sitting opposite each other, wearing their overcoats and scarves. Albert is dealing a hand of cribbage. Harold is blowing on his hands, which are freezing cold. Albert finishes dealing and cuts the deck of cards. Harold tries to turn the top card up. He has difficulty because he is wearing gauntlets. He turns up the top card, an eight.

There is a radio on the table which is playing dance music, softly. They pick up their cards, six each, and sort them out, Harold having difficulty because of his gauntlets. He throws the cards down in anger.

Harold: Oh, it's no good, I can't play cards with these on.
Albert: Take them off, then.
Harold: If I do that my fingers'll be inside them. Gorblimey it's worse than the Russian Front, this house is. What's the time? (*Looks at his watch*) Come on, you've had your ten minutes. It's my turn.
    (*Albert reaches down and picks up the electric fire. He passes it across to Harold, who puts it on an empty chair next to him, gingerly takes his gauntlets off and warms his hands, rubbing them together and flexing his fingers*)
Harold: Oooh, the feeling's coming back.
    (*Albert gets up, takes a blanket, sits down again and wraps it round him. They both pick up their hands. They each throw two cards on the table for the 'box'.*

Albert: It's nice of you to stay home and keep me company, Harold.

Harold: I can't afford to go out anywhere, can I? I'm warning you, Dad, if we have another week like this, I'm turning it in. Thirty bob I've made this week. It's cost more than that to run the horse.

Albert: Oh don't worry, something'll turn up.

Harold: Yeah, my toes if we have much more of it. Three weeks it's been like this. All the savings have gone. The money we've got for pawning the television has gone, and the radio keeps going on and off when it feels like it. We've got a pile of bills over there we could paper the room with.

Albert: We could always burn them, get a bit of heat.

Harold: Well, they're not going to get paid, that's for sure. There's no decent grub in the house. My guts has been rumbling all day. Do you know what I've had to eat today? Half a carrot. And I had a fight to get that out of the horse's mouth. That old bird nearly whacked me with her umbrella. 'That's for the horse,' she said. *(Pause)* I've started getting hallucinations. You turned into a chicken ten minutes ago.

Albert: Stop exaggerating.

Harold: You don't know how close it was. If we'd had some stuffing handy it could have been very painful. We've been hard up before, Dad, but this is ridiculous. I haven't had a fag for a fortnight.

Albert: I've got some dog ends you can roll up.

Harold: No, thank you, they're dog ends of previous dog ends. The last time those dog ends were proper fags was Christmas.

Albert: Come on, it's your lead.

(Harold is holding a Jack, nine, seven, King. Albert is holding two sixes and two sevens. The hold card is an eight. Harold lays his nine)

Harold: Nine.

Albert: *(laying a six)* Fifteen for two. *(He pegs himself two)*
    (Harold reacts in disgust. He lays his Jack)

Harold: Twenty-five.

Albert: *(laying his other six)* Thirty-one for two. *(He pegs himself two)*
    (Harold reacts again. He lays his seven)

Harold: Seven.

Albert: *(laying one of his sevens)* Fourteen for two. *(He pegs himself two)*

Harold: Oh gorblimey! *(He lays his King)* Twenty-four.

Albert: *(laying his second seven)* Thirty-one for two and one's three. *(He pegs himself three. He lays his four cards face up on the table)*

Fifteen two, fifteen four, two's six, two's eight, and twelve's twenty. *(He pegs himself twenty)*

Harold: Twenty? *(He looks at Albert's cards)*

Albert: Yeah. Good hand, ain't it?

Harold: You fixed this hand, didn't you? When I went outside for a gipsy's.

Albert: I never touched them, mate. I don't have to. I can beat you without cheating. How many have you got?

(Harold throws his cards down in disgust. He points to two of them)

Harold: Two.

(Albert pegs Harold two)

Albert: My box.

(Albert picks up the four cards in the box and turns them face up. They are a seven, two eights and a nine. Albert laughs triumphantly)

Albert: Fifteen two, fifteen four, fifteen six, and six is twelve, and nine's twenty-one.

Harold: Oh, that's ridiculous.

(Albert pegs twenty-one out and wins the game)

Albert: Home. *(He tots up some figures on a pad)* That's eleven hundred and fifty-four pounds you owe me.

Harold: You'll have to wait. About twenty years. *(He warms his hands on the electric fire again)* Like two packets of fish fingers, they are. Oh gawd, what a life. I wonder what Ted Heath's doing now. *(Looks at his watch)* Yes, he'll be at the Athenaeum now, just finished his dinner, the taste of the Strasbourg goose pâté still competing with the bouquet of the Château Lafite '55. He'll be sitting in front of the fire, lighting up a Romeo and Juliet, warming a balloon of grande fine champagne cognac in his hand *(mimes warming a brandy glass)*, worrying himself sick about the million unemployed. What a farce it all is. Let's turn it in, Dad. I know what we'll do. We'll collect up all the scrap we can find . . .

Albert: Yeah.

Harold: Lead piping, brass, copper, iron . . .

Albert: Yeah.

Harold: Fill all our pockets up with it . . . and jump in the canal.

Albert: Don't talk silly, Harold.

Harold: Why not, it's better than living like this. It wouldn't take long. I'll lay on top of you.

Albert: Harold, don't talk like that. Things will get better, it's always bad at this time of the year. Spring'll be here soon. The light nights will be coming . . .

Harold: Well, I prefer the winter round here – so you can't see the bleeding place.

(Harold gets up and goes over to his optics. They are all empty save for a dribble at the bottom. He goes along the line with his glass getting a thimbleful from each)

Harold: *(officer's voice)* Well, Carruthers; it's well past sundown, time for a chota peg. Pull the flag down, there's a good chap. The Queen, God bless her. *(He drinks)* By heavens, I'll be glad when the rubber's all in and the natives have bounced it down to Kuala Lumpur. Do you know, Carruthers, it's been estimated that from our estate alone we produce enough rubber to make a hundred million prophylactics. Yes, I think we can be proud of what we're doing. Well . . . I think I'll turn in. It's Sunday tomorrow. Must be up nice and early to wash the elephant.

Albert: You don't half talk a load of cobblers at times, don't you?

Harold: *(officer's voice)* It's the sun old boy. I went out this morning without my helmet. *(Reverts to his own voice)* Why couldn't you have been rich? Why couldn't you have owned a rubber plantation instead of a poxy rag and bone yard? I would have fancied myself out there, striding about with my baggy shorts on. I wish I'd stayed out in Malaya when I was in the Army. I had it made out there, and I didn't know it. There was a beautiful Chinese bird who fancied me. Tchin Lo. Her father owned a shipping line or something. Rolling in it, he was. And all I could think about was getting home . . . to this. I must have been off my chump. They were all the same, all the lads. From the rat holes of England, they couldn't wait to get home.

(Harold is now warming his hands in front of the electric fire again)

Albert: Best country in the world, this is.

Harold: Don't give me that. It's cold, it's wet, it's miserable, it's expensive, it's crowded, the pubs shut early . . .

Suddenly all the lights go out in the room. There is just the glow of the radio set. The electric fire fades away)

Harold: . . . and the bleeding lights keep going out.

Albert: The meter's run out. Have you got a shilling?

Harold: I told you, I'm skint. I've got about three and a half pence on me.

Albert: Well, I ain't got any. We'll have to put one of them foreign coins in it again.

Harold: That meter holds more stocks of foreign currency than the Bank of England.

Albert: Them French francs fit nice. Where are they?

Harold: In the sideboard.

(*Albert goes over to the sideboard and rummages around. He lights a candle*)

Harold: This is BBC Radio Two. Here is the news. Last month Britain's International currency reserves climbed to an all-time high when the electricity meter at 24 Oil Drum Lane, Shepherd's Bush was emptied. Our Financial Correspondent says . . .

(*From the radio the music stops, and an announcer comes on*)

Announcer: This is Radio London bringing you an up-to-the-minute news flash.

(*Harold turns up the volume*)

Albert: Stop acting the maggot.

Harold: It's not me. It's for real.

Announcer: Earlier this evening two prisoners made a daring escape from Wormwood Scrubs in West London. The men are John Edward Spooner, aged thirty-eight, and Frank Arthur Ferris, aged sixty-four. Both men were serving seven years for armed robbery. The two men are considered to be dangerous and should not be approached by the general public. If sighted you should immediately contact the local police station. And now back to Harold Macmillan, his electric guitar and the Hawaiian Five, broadcasting to you live from the Copacabana Rooms in Catford. Take it away, Harold.

(*The music starts again. Harold switches it off. Albert is lighting matches at the sideboard*)

Albert: I don't know why they don't leave the gate open down that Scrubs, they're always getting out. We ought to have our rates reduced, it's dangerous living round here.

Harold: Hurry up and find that money. I'm freezing.

Albert: There's no francs here.

Harold: Let me have a look. (*He goes over. He bumps into a chair, knocks the fire over. He yells with pain*) Oh, my bleeding shin! (*He reaches the sideboard*)

Albert: There's a Yugoslavian one here with a hole in the middle.

Harold: I've got a leg here with a dent in the middle. That'll do.

Albert: No it won't. It's too small.

(*Harold rummages around the drawer. There is a loud knocking at the front door*)

Albert: Who's that at this time of night?

Harold: I clean forgot. It's Prince Philip. I invited him round for supper. He's always on the ear'ole. How should I know who it is? Go and see. I'll do this.

(Albert picks his way across the room and goes into the hall. Harold rummages round amongst the coins)

Harold: Escudos, no they're no good. Five guilders . . . Too big. Pfennigs. They look the right size. *(He goes to the meter and puts the coin in. The lights come on again. Harold turns round)* That's good news, twenty pfennigs fits perfectly, now we . . . *(He freezes)*

(The two escaped prisoners are standing at the door, Spooner with his hand covering Albert's mouth. Albert is petrified. Spooner is holding a lump of lead pipe)

Spooner: One move and the old man gets it.

Harold: Who are you, what are you doing here?

Ferris: Do as you're told and nobody'll get hurt.

Spooner: Is there anybody else here?

(Albert shakes his head frantically)

Harold: No, just me and my dad. Let him go. *(He advances. Spooner raises the pipe above the old man's head. Harold stops)* Don't hit him. He's an old man.

Spooner: Then don't try anything. *(He lets go of Albert and pushes him over to Harold. Albert stands next to Harold, shaking with fear)* Frank, go and have a look around.

(Ferris goes out of the room. Spooner walks across to the window and has a furtive look behind the curtains)

Harold: You're the two blokes who've escaped from the Scrubs.

Spooner: Clever boy. You heard it on the radio, did you?

Harold: Yeah. About five minutes ago.

Spooner: Did they say we were dangerous?

Albert: Yeah.

Spooner: Well, they're right. We are. Very. So watch it. If you play your cards right, nothing will happen to you. All right?

(Albert and Harold nod. Ferris comes back into the room)

Ferris: No, there's no one here.

Spooner: Right. Now we understand each other we can behave like civilized human beings.

Harold: What do you want with us?

Spooner: I'll tell you. First of all, we want some grub, we're starving.

Harold: So are we.

Spooner: Look, sonny, don't try and be funny. Grandad – out in the kitchen, bring some grub in. And don't try anything otherwise pretty boy here will have a slight indentation in his nut. And hurry up.

(Albert nods and hurries off)

Spooner: Give us the keys of your car.

Harold: Car? What car? We haven't got a car.

Spooner: Come off it, everybody's got a car.

Harold: We haven't.

Spooner: You've got a garage out there.

Harold: That's not a garage, that's the stables.

Spooner: What? You mean an 'orse?

Harold: Yeah. We're rag and bone men, that's the only transport we've got.

Ferris: We can't make a getaway on an 'orse, Johnny.

Harold: Dick Turpin did.

Spooner: Look, sonny, you're beginning to aggravate me, I've had enough of you already.

Ferris: What are we going to do, Johnny? They haven't got a car. We'll get caught.

Spooner: Shut up, will you? Have you got a telephone?

Harold: Yes.

Spooner: Right. *(To Ferris)* Ring Margie up, tell her where we are and tell her to get a car over here.

Harold: You can't do that.

Spooner: Why?

Harold: We couldn't pay the bill. It's been cut off.

Spooner: I know something else that'll be cut off.

Harold: There's a public call box at the end of the street.

Spooner: We can't go down there, can we – the place is crawling with law. How much money have you got in the house?

Harold: Not much. We've had a bad week you see, trade has been very slack lately.

Spooner: How much? Turn your pockets out. *(Harold turns his pockets out and puts three and a half pence on the table)* Three and a half pence!

Harold: My dad might have a couple of bob hidden away.

Spooner: I don't believe it. *(He grabs Harold by the lapels)* Look, if you're lying I don't fancy your chances of waking up in the morning.

Harold: I'm not lying. We're skint. There's some foreign money in the electric meter – I mean, if you was thinking of getting out of the country, it might come in handy. There's pfennigs and francs . . . perhaps you could change them at the bank.

Spooner: *(letting go of Harold)* Gorblimey, of all the houses round here we have to pick this one. No money, no car, no telephone. 'That's a likely looking house, Johnny, let's go in there, we'll be all right there.' Berk!

Ferris: It wasn't my fault.

Spooner: No, it was my fault. I shouldn't have brought you. I should have gone on my own. I could have been miles away by now. *(To Harold)* He got his bleeding trousers caught on the barbed wire. I had to go back up the wall and get him down. He's been holding me up ever since we got away. He's too old, he can't keep up with me. He can't run 'cos he's got bad legs, he's a right liability.

Harold: Yeah, I know how you feel. It's the same with me.

Spooner: We wouldn't have been caught doing the job in the first place if it hadn't been for him.

Harold: Really?

Spooner: Yeah. We got in the vaults like good 'uns. We could have had it away on our toes – of course, he goes potty, stuffs all his pockets with gold bullion, he couldn't move. Rooted to the spot, he was. Too weak, you see, too old – he's gone.

Harold: Yeah. It's like him out there. Held me back all my life, he has.

Spooner: Yeah. You're better off on your own.

Harold: You can say that again.

(Albert comes in carrying a tray of food)

Albert: Here we are. I'm afraid this is all we've got, sir. *(He puts the tray down on the table. Ferris and Spooner eagerly go over to it. Spooner's face falls when he sees it)*

Spooner: What's this?

Albert: Er . . . that's cold porridge . . . from this morning. No milk, I'm afraid. That's bread, and that's cheese. You can scrape the green bits off.

(Spooner bangs the bread against the plate. It is rock hard. The plate breaks)

Spooner: We can't eat that. That's disgusting. There'd be a riot if they served that in prison.

Albert: That's all we've got.

Spooner: *(to Harold)* You don't have to eat this, do you?

Harold: *(nods)* Well, lately, yes.

Spooner: You poor bastard. You'd be better off inside.

Ferris: I'll eat it. *(To Albert)* Thank you very much.

Spooner: Ugh, gawd, you'd eat anything, wouldn't you? He's got no taste, no finesse. Oi!! (*Ferris is eating the porridge*) I don't know how I got tied up with you. We've got nothing in common. Nothing at all.

Ferris: The trouble with you is you've had it too easy. I was brought up in the Depression. You ate what you could get.

Albert: Yeah, that's right, I remember them days. They don't know what it's all about, these kids, do they?

Ferris: That's for sure. They don't know how lucky they are.

Albert: They don't know they're born. I worked my fingers to the bone for him when he was little. He don't appreciate it.

Ferris: No, none of them do.

(*Spooner and Harold exchange 'Here we go again' looks*)

Harold: (*to Spooner*) The bread might be all right if I toasted it.

Spooner: No, no, that's all right. Don't bother.

Harold: If you'd come a couple of weeks ago, you would have been all right. We do quite well normally. It's just you've come at the wrong time.

Spooner: I'm sorry. I just couldn't get away. Oh, it's not your fault. Have you got any restaurants round here?

Harold: Yes. There's two Chinese, two Indians, two Pakistanis, and a Bangladesh.

Spooner: No English restaurants?

Harold: No, there's not much call for them round here. There's only the two of us.

Spooner: I'll tell you what, you nip down to the Chinese and bring back a Mandarin dinner for four.

Albert: We haven't got any money.

Spooner: Put it on the slate.'

Harold: They put the bar up three weeks ago. I couldn't get a box of matches on tick round here.

Spooner: Oh blimey, I think I'll give myself up. (*He wanders across the room. As he passes the skeleton . . .*) Who's this – the lodger? (*He reaches the goldfish bowl. He watches the goldfish*) What are they liked grilled?

Harold: Oh no, not Charlie. You can't eat Charlie. He's not as big as he looks. He's magnified. He's only that size really. (*Measures a couple of inches with his fingers*)

Spooner: I was only joking. I only eat fish on a Friday as it happens. (*He takes a packet of cigarettes out of his pocket and lights one*)

Harold: Er . . . excuse me. Do you think I might have one of them?

Spooner: This is a week's wages where I've just come from.

Harold: Oh yes, of course, I'm sorry.

Spooner: Oh, all right. Here, have the packet, I've got some more. (*He gives Harold the packet. Harold takes a cigarette. Spooner gives him a light. Harold inhales luxuriously. Ferris is golloping his food*)

Ferris: Here, this is good, Johnny. He cooks a fair drop of porridge.

Albert: I'm sorry we haven't got any more milk. We had the last drop in the tea this morning.

Ferris: That's all right, it's going down a treat, this is.

Albert: It's not too lumpy for you?

Ferris: No, I like lumps. (*He licks the spoon*)

Spooner: (*wincing*) Oh, he's got some disgusting habits, he really has.

Harold: You should see him. (*Indicates Albert*) Your bloke's got manners like Anna Neagle compared with him.

Spooner: Five years I've had to put up with him. Five years in the same cell. He eats like a pig. Stuck with him day and night. No escape from it. Five years.

Harold: You're lucky. I've done thirty-nine.

Spooner: That's why I had to get out. I couldn't stand it any more. I didn't mind prison – it was him.

Harold: Wouldn't they give you a transfer?

Spooner: No, sadistic they are. I couldn't even escape on me own. He insisted on coming with me. Said he'd blow the gaff if I didn't take him. I can't get away from him.

Harold: What are you going to do now?

Spooner: I've got no choice, have I. Everything's gone for the chop. I had intended breaking in here, pinching some grub, robbing you of all your money, taking your car and off. That's all gone for a toss, ain't it?

Harold: Are you going to stay for the night?

Spooner: No, we've got to get as far away from this area as possible. (*He goes over to Ferris*) Come on, you, on your feet. We're going.

Ferris: No, I can't go tonight. I'm exhausted.

Spooner: What do you mean, exhausted, we've only come bleeding five hundred yards (*To Harold*) See what I mean? He's worse than an iron ball round your leg, he is.

Ferris: I can't go any further, let's go in the morning. I've got to rest up.

Spooner: We can't rest every five hundred yards, it'll take us a week to do two miles. This is going to be the slowest getaway in history.

Albert: Don't talk to him like that. He's an old man. It's not his fault.

Harold: Why don't you mind your own business for once?

Albert: He can't help being old.

Harold: Then he shouldn't have escaped, should he? He should have stayed where he was. Given him a chance.

Albert: He's just as entitled to escape as he is.

Harold: He didn't have to go with him, did he? Holding him back ... He could have gone on his own. He could have gone up Du Cane Road, and he could have gone up Scrubs Lane.

Albert: Oh yes, I know, that's what you would have done, ain't it? You wouldn't have even got my trousers off the barbed wire. You would have left me hanging there.

Harold: I bloody would, too. And rang the alarm bell. I wouldn't have taken you with me.

Albert: Oh, I know that. I wouldn't expect any consideration from you. You just think of yourself. You've got to paddle your own canoe in this world.

Harold: Paddle your own canoe! You threw your paddle away thirty years ago when I left school. You've spent your life laying in the back with the gramophone on. You've done nothing to help me. Nothing.

Albert: I pull my weight.

Harold: Yeah. All six stone of it. I know just how he feels. It's like having a millstone round your neck. One step forward and two back.

Albert: *(to Ferris)* See, that's the sort of thing I have to put up with. That's my son.

Ferris: I know, mate, they're all the same. When you get old they don't want to know you.

Albert: Oh, you don't have to tell me that. They don't let you forget it, either. I lead a life of drudgery here. I'd be better off dead.

Harold: Hear hear.

Ferris: It's the same with him. I taught that boy everything he knows. He was nothing when I found him.

Spooner: I wasn't in bleeding jail, was I? *(To Harold)* I was straight, I was. I was a bank clerk – till he opened an account.

Ferris: Yeah, I sussed you out, didn't I? I could see you had the makings. I knew you was a crook as soon as I saw you behind them bars.

Spooner: Yeah, and I've been behind them ever since, ain't I? Worst day's work I ever did, getting tied up with you. I might have been a branch manager by now. Ruined my life, he has.

Harold: So's he. It's just the same.

Albert: I ain't no crook.

Harold: You're worse. You're a ponce. You've been sucking the life blood out of me for years. Dracula would have been a better father than you. At least he only had a go at night, you're at it all day long. I've never had a chance.

Albert: Never had a chance – what could you have been?

Harold: Anything. I've got brains. I've just never had a chance to use them. I wanted to be a doctor, he wouldn't let me.

Albert: Well, that's saved a few lives, ain't it?

(Albert laughs, nudges Ferris, and he joins in)

Spooner: What you you laughing at? That's not funny. That's tragic, that is. He could have been eminent by now. He might have had a string of abortion clinics.

Harold: Euthanasia might be more useful.

Spooner: Yeah, I know what you mean.

Albert: You'll be as old as us one day. You won't be so cocky about euthanasia then. You'll be passing bricks, you will.

Harold: If it means being a liability like you are, I don't want to live that long.

Ferris: Don't you talk to your father like that. Show a bit of respect.

Spooner: You mind your own bleeding business.

Ferris: And you can keep a civil tongue in your head.

Spooner: Oh yeah?

Ferris: Yeah.

Albert: Yeah.

Harold: Yeah.

(The four of them are now standing – the two young ones facing the two old ones, belligerently. Suddenly there is the sound of a police siren in the distance. They all freeze. Spooner and Ferris are frightened. Spooner runs to the window and peeks out behind the curtain. The siren gets nearer and nearer and then fades away into the distance. Ferris clutches his heart)

Ferris: Oh my gawd.

Spooner: Right, that's it. I'm off.

Ferris: No, no Johnny – Johnny, you can't go without me.

Spooner: We stand a better chance on our own.

Ferris: No, Johnny, we've always been together, you can't leave me now.

Spooner: I've got to. The law are looking for two of us. They know we travel together. We've got to split up. Travel at our own speed, it's the only way.

Ferris: I'll never make it on my own, Johnny. I've got nowhere to go. I haven't got any friends. I'll get caught.

Spooner: We'll both get caught if we stay together.

Ferris: No, we won't.

Spooner: We will. You can't move as fast as me. Look – there's a thousand quid in the locker at Waterloo Station. It's yours. You can have the lot. But just leave me on my own – give me a chance.

Ferris: Johnny . . .

Albert: You can't leave him.

Harold: He's got to, hasn't he? Stands to reason. He's got a much better chance on his own.

Albert: And what about him?

Harold: Well . . . (*He shrugs*)

Albert: Exactly. It don't matter about him, does it? 'Cos he's old.

Harold: Well, all right, so that's life. Survival of the fittest. The weak go to the wall. It's like birds migrating. If you can't keep up you fall in the sea. That's all there is to it.

Albert: That's not all there is to it. He ain't a bird, he's a human being. There's supposed to be honour amongst thieves. Butch Cassidy and the Sundance Kid stayed together, didn't they? Right to the end.

Harold: He ain't no Sundance Kid, is he? He'd have a job doing a slow waltz. (*To Spooner*) You go on, do yourself a favour, get out while you've got the chance. You've done enough for him. I wish I was going with you.

Spooner: Well . . . cheerio, Frank.

Ferris: Don't leave me, Johnny. I don't stand a chance on my own. You know that.

Harold: Don't listen to him. I've heard that all my life.

Ferris: I won't last five minutes without you. I'm no good on my own. Stay with me. I won't be a lumber to you, honest.

Harold: Don't fall for it.

Ferris: I haven't got much longer to go anyway. My heart's not what it was.

Harold: Oh no. Not that one.

Ferris: Take me with you . . . please. Please.

Harold: Don't. Don't.

(Spooner hesitates. Finally he nods)

Spooner: All right . . . come on.

Albert: Good boy – well done.

Spooner: *(to Harold)* What can you do?

Harold: Yeah, I know.

Spooner: Well . . . cheerio. *(They shake hands)* Thanks for everything.

Harold: Well, it wasn't much was it?

Spooner: Would you like to come and visit us?

Harold: Well, I don't know . . . where?

Spooner: Where else – Wormwood Scrubs. I stand no chance, do I? It'll either be tonight or tomorrow, why prolong the agony? *(To Ferris)* Come on, you, if we hurry up, we'll be back in time for supper.

(Albert shakes hands with Ferris)

Ferris: Cheerio.

Albert: Cheerio, look after yourself.

Ferris: And you. *(Indicates Spooner)* He's not a bad lad, is he?

Albert: No. *(Indicates Harold)* Neither's he, really.

Ferris: *(picks up the lead pipe)* He wouldn't really have hit you with this.

Albert: No. Cheerio, then. I'll bring you some porridge on visiting day.

Ferris: Oh, thanks. Don't forget to leave the lumps in.

Albert: No, all right.

(The lights go out)

Harold: Oh gorblimey, them pfennigs don't last long, do they? Dad, have we got any more pfennigs?

Albert: No, that was the last one.

Harold: Johnny?

Spooner: Yeah?

Harold: Can you lend me a shilling for the meter?

Spooner: Yeah, I think I've got one here somewhere. It's the only one I've got. You're welcome to it.

Harold: Thanks. I'll give it back to you on Sunday. *(He goes over to the meter, puts the coin in, the lights come on again. Ferris and Spooner have gone)*

Albert: They've gone.

Harold: Yeah.

Albert: I'm glad they stayed together.

Harold: *(nodding gloomily)* Yeah, I expect you are. Oh well, I suppose I'd better go and lock the cage up.

(Harold and Albert go out into the hall and lock the front door. Film clip of Ferris and Spooner in their cell and a warder locking the door.

Our final view is of Harold and Albert starting another game of cards)

Christmas 1973

First transmission 24 December 1973

Christmas 1973 featured
Frank Thornton as The Travel Agency Assistant
with Arnold Diamond and Mary Barclay
and was produced by Graeme Muir

SCENE 1
Harold is driving the horse and cart along a street. They stop,
and Harold ties up the horse to a parking meter. He puts a coin
in.

SCENE 2
The Steptoes' lounge. Albert is sitting huddled up in his overcoat making home-made paper chains.

SCENE 3
A travel agency, furnished with a counter and some chairs.
There are travel posters on the wall, brochures on racks, leaflets
on the counter, where a middle-aged, middle-class couple are
browsing through some literature. A male assistant is on the
telephone.

Assistant: Oh, that's fine, Charles. I'll confirm it in writing.
　　Ciao. (*Replaces phone*) Well, that's that.
Man: We're in?
Assistant: Yes. One double room with bath, balcony overlooking
　　the sea. The Hotel Miramar, Puerto de Vallarta, Majorca. That's
　　for the whole of the Christmas period, returning to the UK
　　January 3rd.
Man: Good. Now, I see there's a golf course attached. Is that a
　　separate charge?

Assistant: Yes, I'm afraid it is. But you can pay here, save spending the old pesetas. If you care to look through the brochure you'll find quite a few extras – car hire, sailing, tours, night clubs – they can all be paid for in this country. If you'd care to make a note of anything you'd like, we'd be pleased to make the arrangements for you.

Man: Thank you.

(They start going through the brochure. The door opens and Harold comes in. He is in his working clothes. He goes up to the counter. The assistant looks at him with distaste)

Assistant: Excuse me. *(He goes over to Harold)* The dustbins are round the back in the alleyway. Please don't come into the shop again. *(He moves back to the other customers)* Now, how are we getting along?

Man: This hotel. It's all right, is it? I mean, there's a lot of . . . er . . . working class going to Majorca these days.

Assistant: Not to the Miramar, I assure you, sir. Thirty-two acres in its own grounds, own swimming pool, own beach – oh no, you'll be well away from them. They have guard dogs as well.

(Harold reacts)

Man: Oh well, that's all right, then.

(Harold moves along the counter until he is standing next to the two customers. He tries to attract the assistant's attention)

Woman: I see they have a beauty salon and a hairdresser.

Assistant: Oh yes, yes, first class. International standard.

Woman: Is there a sauna?

Assistant: Oh, yes. I think you'll find they have everything there that they have in Epsom.

(Harold is now looking over the woman's shoulder at the brochure. She sniffs and realizes he is there. She looks round at him. She looks at her husband. He looks at Harold. Harold smiles. They edge away from him, sniffing. Harold is puzzled. He looks down at his boots. They are covered in horse dung)

Harold: Oh, I do beg your pardon. *(To the assistant)*. You'd think they'd be used to that, living in Epsom.

Assistant: Look, what do you want?

Harold: I want the same as they want. A bit of service. I'm going on holiday, ain't I?

Assistant: Are you? Well, I'm afraid we don't do holiday camps. There's a perfectly good place in Oxford Street, if you'd like to—

Harold: Who's talking about holiday camps?

Assistant: We only do de luxe first-class holidays.

Harold: That's right, that's what I'm going on. You don't remember me, do you?

Assistant: Should I?

Harold: Well, you booked me in. You took me bleeding deposit quick enough. Steptoe. I've come to pay the balance.

Assistant: Steptoe?

Harold: Harold. I've got my horse on a meter outside. Could you get a wiggle on, please?

Assistant: *(thumbing through file)* Steptoe. Steptoe. *(Finds it)* Ah. Yes. Oh dear. *(Takes him a little way down the counter)* Is this right, the Hotel Miramar?

Harold: That's right, the Hotel Miramar. Puerto de Vallarta. *(The couple look up at this, and look at Harold, aghast)* A double room with bath, balcony, overlooking the sea. Ten days, including Christmas.

Assistant: Yes, yes, that's quite right.

Harold: Unfortunately there's been a change of plan.

Assistant: *(brightening up)* You can't go. You want to cancel. Certainly, sir, I'll just . . .

Harold: Oh no, I'm going. It's just that I'll be going on my own. You will notice that I had originally booked for myself and a young lady friend.

Assistant: Yes?

Harold: Regretfully I found out this morning that the said young lady in question has decided to give me the elbow. But I'll still keep the same room. No doubt I'll pick something up out there.

(The couple exchange looks)

Man: Excuse me, did I hear you say you were staying at the Hotel Miramar in Puerto de Vallarta?

Harold: Yes, that's right. Are you going there as well?

Man: Er . . . yes.

Harold: Oh, that's wonderful. My name is Steptoe. *(He wipes his hand on his coat and offers it. The man looks at it and hesitantly starts to bring his hand up. His wife hurriedly puts a brochure into his hand)* I'm staying in Room 23. What room are you in?

Man: *(looks at his itinerary, worried)* Twenty-four.

Harold: Oh, that is good news. We could have breakfast together on the balcony.

Woman: *(flustered)* Oh well, I don't know, I . . .

Harold: Oh don't worry, I do wear pyjamas when I'm on holiday, I assure you. I mean, you have to in these Spanish hotels, you never know when they're going to fall down, do you? *(He laughs)* It wouldn't do to be dug out of the rubble in the nude, would it? Er . . . oosted ahblah Español?

Woman: Sí, poco.

Harold: Moi aussi. I've been taking lessons at the Shepherd's Bush Adult Further Education classes. Excellent teacher. He's a Pakistani. His English isn't too hot, but his Spanish – excellente. He was first rowed ashore in Barcelona, I think that explains it. He thought it was Dungeness. Well now, if you will excuse me, I must just pay my bill. I don't like to leave my horse too long. She gets very impatient. It wouldn't do to have her kick some poor parking warden up the Black Hole of Calcutta, would it? *(To assistant)* Er – how much do I owe you?

Assistant: That's, er . . . ninety-eight pounds to pay.

Harold: Certainly, and very reasonable. This is going to be the best Christmas I've ever spent. Especially now I'm going to be among friends.

(They give him a sickly smile. Harold takes a load of filthy dirty, creased banknotes from various pockets and puts them on the counter. The assistant eyes them with great distaste)

Harold: I must apologize for the condition they're in. They do pass through some very mucky hands in my business. Not everybody's as particular as I am. Would you mind counting them for me? *(The assistant starts to count. He licks his finger, grimaces, gets sponge from desk and counts notes)* I've got some more here somewhere. *(Takes a newspaper parcel from his coat pocket, opens it. Reveals four great doorstep sandwiches)* Oh gawd, me lunch. I'd better not take them home, my old man will go potty. Bung them in your waste-paper basket, will you? Unless, of course, you would care to partake? *(He offers the couple his sandwiches)*

Man: No, thank you.

Harold: It's Polish sausage. A bit chewy, but very nourishing.

Man: Thank you, no.

(The assistant hands Harold one filthy note back, holding it by the extreme corner)

Assistant: One too many.

Harold: No, no, no, you can keep that. You have been most helpful, squire.

Assistant: You are too kind. Your tickets.

Harold: *(takes them)* Thank you. Well, I'll bid you good day, then. I shall look forward to seeing you in Puerto de Vallarta. Or we might meet on the plane. I'll save you a couple of seats. *(Hands the sandwiches to the assistant)* Have them for your tea. Silly to be proud. It's a pity to waste them. Good afternoon. *(Raises his cap to the woman)* I shall look forward to having a good old-knees-up on Christmas Day. We'll show them Spaniards what dancing's all about, eh?

(There is a loud horse whinny. Harold goes to the door)

Harold: *(shouting)* All right, I'm coming. *(To couple)* Vaya con Dios . . . *(Horse whinnies again. Harold opens the door)* Shut up, you great bad-tempered pillock! *(He shuts the door behind him)*

(The man and woman go up to the counter)

Man: Er . . . we've changed our mind. I think we'll go to Bournemouth instead.

(They go hurriedly)

Assistant: *(to himself)* I don't blame you! *(He drops the sandwiches into the wastepaper basket)*

SCENE 4
The lounge. There are home-made paper chains stretching from each corner to the light. Albert is sitting at the table in his overcoat making more chains from coloured strips of paper. He is singing as he works.

Albert: Enoch's dreaming of a White Christmas, just like the ones he used to know . . . de da da da da da . . . *(He finishes the chain, gathers it up and goes to the door)*

SCENE 5
The hall. Albert crosses the hall and goes out into the yard.

SCENE 6
The yard. Albert crosses the yard and goes into the outside lavatory.

SCENE 7
The lavatory. It is partially decorated with chains, holly and mistletoe. Albert hangs up the new chain on a couple of nails,

standing on the seat to do so. From a cardboard box he takes some sheets of Christmas wrapping paper, folds them and cuts along the fold. He gathers the sheets together, removes the squares of newspaper from the hook and hangs the wrapping paper in their place.

Albert: Oh yes, very festive. Bit shiny, but nice. (*He takes out a holly wreath*) Now, where shall I put this? (*Tries it on the wall above the lavatory*) Yeah, that's nice. (*He takes a nail, puts it against the wall, hits thumb with hummer. The nail falls down loo. Albert tries to retrieve it, fails*) Oh cobblers. I'll hang it up later. (*He picks up his box and goes out into the yard and back into the house*)

SCENE 8
The lounge. Albert enters, puts down the box, and takes out a paper hat. He puts it on the skeleton's head, and puts a cigar in its mouth.

Albert: There you are – John Gregson. Just the tree, and that's it.

SCENE 9
The hall. Albert goes into hall and drags a small Christmas tree from a cupboard under the stairs. It is completely devoid of needles. He takes it back into the lounge.

SCENE 10
The lounge.

Albert: We'll have to think about getting a new one next year. Still, it'll save sweeping up afterwards. (*He rummages around in the box and comes up with a tatty old fairy with one leg*) Blimey, I think you've seen more Christmases than I have, girl (*He blows the dust off the fairy and clips it on to the top of the tree. He straightens her dress out*) There you go, your first Common Market Christmas. Good, ain't it? You and me, we remember the bad old days, don't we? Bloody sight better off than we are now. Do you remember your first Christmas? 1932. Harold was six months old. I bought you for him. Do you remember? He kept gurgling and pointing up at you, so I lifted him up and he stretched out his chubby little fist, grabbed hold of you – and pulled your leg off. We never did find it, did we? I think he ate it. You've watched him grow up, haven't you? You and me. From that little baby boy right the way up to what he is now. A bleeding disappointment, ain't he? *(He gets tinsel out of box)* You've seen some Christmases stuck up there, haven't you? Some good, some bad. Remember Christmas 1936? Just after his mother was took from us. Very sudden it was. Two days before Christmas. I'd already bought her present, as well – that was a waste of money. They were pretty miserable Christmases after that. Up until 1940. That was a good 'un. Except for the blitz. Still, if it hadn't been for that I wouldn't have had the ATS girl from the barrage balloon site billeted on me. What was her name? Anne MacFaddern. *(Chuckles)* You never saw much of me that Christmas, did you? Dear oh dear, what a big girl she was. If they'd stuck her up on the end of a cable she would have brought down half the Luftwaffe. We nearly got killed in that blitz, me and Harold, remember? She thought she heard a bomb coming and she threw herself on top of us. Yeah ... if it hadn't been for the rationing I would have married her. Never mind, I've still got Harold, that's a blessing. Always spends Christmas with me, he's a good boy. I couldn't bear to spend it on my own, not at my age. Yes, I've got a lot to be thankful for. He'll be coming home in a minute. I'd better go and switch the yard light on.

SCENE 11

The yard. Albert switches the yard light on. He is just about to go in when there is a yell of pain from Harold. The yell comes from the lavatory.

Albert: Harold! Is that you? Harold? Where are you? Harold?
  (The lavatory door slowly opens. Harold emerges, holding his backside with one hand, the holly wreath in the other. He holds the wreath up and looks at it. Albert goes over to him)
Albert: Oh Harold, I'm sorry, you didn't—
Harold: Yes, I did. From a height of about two feet. *(He winces in pain and rubs his backside)*
Albert: I'm sorry, it was part of my decorations.
Harold: So am I now. What did you want to put it on the seat for?

Albert: I forgot it was there. I was going to hang it up on the wall. Are you in pain?

Harold: Of course I'm in pain. So would you be with a bum full of perforations. (*He winces again and rubs his backside*)

Albert: Never mind. Come inside. I'll fill up a bowl of hot water and put a sprig of mint in it, then you can sit in it.

Harold: Oh, leave me alone.

Albert: I've finished the decorations. They look very nice. I think you'll be pleased with them.

Harold: Oh. Yes. Well, I wanted to have a word with you about . . .

Albert: I haven't blown the balloons up. I'll leave them to you. I can't manage them these days. Me lungs aren't what they used to be. I can't even inflate the tit on the end of the sausage ones . . . (*They enter the hall*) We must have balloons, Christmas ain't the same without balloons. (*He slams the door, just missing Harold's backside. Harold winces. Albert goes into the lounge. Harold hobbles after him*)

SCENE 12
The lounge. Albert comes in, followed by Harold.

Albert: There you are. What do you think? (*He points at the pathetic decorations*)

Harold: (*looking round*) Oh yes, that's very colourful, Dad. Very nice.

Albert: Dolly looks nice on top of the tree, don't she?

Harold: Yes. Yes, she does.

Albert: Lasted well, ain't she? Forty-one years now. It wouldn't be the same without her, would it?

Harold: Dad, I want to have a talk with you . . . about Christmas.

Albert: I know, we've still got a lot to do. So we'd better get organized. I haven't ordered the turkey. They're too expensive yet. I thought if we waited till Christmas Eve I'll nip down the market and get one at the auction.

Harold: Dad, before you go on . . . (*He sits, and rises immediately with a howl. Albert puts a cushion under him*)

Albert: I'll leave you to get the vegetables, 'cos I can't hump them about, not with my back. You can pick them up on the cart. I've ordered the fruits and nuts, and I've asked him to put in a big box of dates, because I know you like dates. I've got the crackers, look. (*Shows him a box of crackers. He takes out one and, holding it to his ear, shakes it*) They're good ones, good presents inside them. Little whistles, and them things you move about till you've got all the little balls in the holes. You like them, don't you? You're always playing with them.

Harold: Dad, sit down, I've got to talk to you.

Albert: Now, booze. There's what we've got here and I thought I'd get a crate of brown ale, a crate of light ale, a bottle of Tom Thumb, a bottle of gold watch, and a bottle of Vera Lynn, in case the vicar comes. Do you want any wine?

Harold: Dad, will you please . . .

Albert: 'Cos if you do they're knocking out some Dago Red down the supermarket. Eighty-one pee a litre. I don't know if that's the price, or the effect it has on you. (*He laughs. Harold smiles weakly*) I started boiling the puddings this morning, can you smell them? (*He sniffs*)

Harold: (*sniffing*) They smell wonderful.

Albert: They're nice dark ones. Black as a gorilla's goolies, they are. I've put half a quid's worth of tanners in. I'll make sure you get one this year. Now the point is, do you want mince pies or not?

Harold: Dad, I won't be here.

Albert: 'Cos if you do, say so now, I don't want to mess about . . . (*he slows down and tails off as he realizes what Harold has said*) . . . making . . . them . . . on . . . Christmas morning. What did you say?

Harold: I said, I won't be here.

Albert: Of course you'll be here, it's Christmas.

Harold: No. I'm going away this Christmas.

Albert: Going away?

Harold: Yeah.

Albert: Where?

Harold: Puerto de Vallarta.

Albert: Where the bleeding hell's that?

Harold: Majorca.

Albert: Majorca? We don't want to go to Majorca.

Harold: I didn't say we, I said me. I'm going on my own.

Albert: (*sitting down*) On your own?

Harold: Yes.

Albert: Without me?

Harold: Yes.

Albert: Without me?

Harold: Without you.

Albert: On your own?

Harold: On my own. *(Albert mouths 'On your own?')* Yes! I would have told you before, but I wasn't sure whether I could raise sufficient conkers, but this morning I managed to pay off the balance. So I'm off.

Albert: I don't understand, Harold. You always spend Christmas here with me, just the two of us, together.

Harold: I know, that's why I'm going to Majorca on my own. Look, Dad, I'll be perfectly honest, I can't spend another Christmas stuck in this rat hole with you. Over forty years I've done it. Year after year after year. If I do it just once more I shall go bonkers.

Albert: I thought you enjoyed it.

Harold: Dad, how can you say that? We don't enjoy it. We've never enjoyed it.

Albert: I enjoy it.

Harold: Liar. You only enjoy seeing me miserable. It's the same thing every time, we go through the same ritual every year. I sit there for three solid days with a daft paper hat stuck on my head, watching you sat in front of the goggle box, walnut shells, tangerine skins and fag ash piling up all round your boots. If it wasn't for the occasional calls of nature I'll swear blind you'd be buried alive by Boxing Day. It's soul destroying, Dad, I can't stand it any more.

Albert: I didn't realize you felt like that.

Harold: Well, you should do. I tell you every year. You just don't listen, do you? Chomping away on them nuts all day, and the telly up full blast, you don't hear anything, do you?

Albert: It's not like that all day. What about the present-giving? That's a nice part of the day.

Harold: It is, yes, I agree. All of thirty seconds, that takes up. Here's yours, where's mine? Open it, Harold. Cor, just what I wanted, three handkerchiefs and a pair of Y-fronts.

Albert: How did you know?

Harold: How did I know? 'Cos that's what I always get. I've had three handkerchiefs and a pair of Y-fronts for the past twenty-five years.

Albert: You're getting very cynical, Harold, you never used to be like that. It's not the present, it's the thought behind it.

Harold: Yeah, like 'How cheap can I get away with it this year?'

Albert: You're getting very cruel, as well. I buy you the best presents I can afford.

Harold: *(relents)* Yeah, I know. I'm not knocking the presents. It's just that I've got to get away this year, that's all. Well, gorblimey, I spend fifty-one weeks of the year with you, surely you don't begrudge me ten days?

Albert: Ten days? You're going to be away for ten days?

Harold: Well, there's no point in going all that way just for Christmas dinner, is there?

Albert: You mean that we won't be seeing in the New Year together either?

Harold: No, not this year.

Albert: We always see the New Year in together.

Harold: Yeah, I know. Perhaps that's why we have such rotten years. Perhaps if we don't see 1974 in it might not turn out so bad.

Albert: So you've got yourself all sorted out?

Harold: Yes.

Albert: I expect it's too much to suppose that you've thought about what I'm going to do?

Harold: That's where you're wrong. I've got you all organized. That was the first thing I did. I've had a word with the vicar . . .

Albert: Oh gawd.

Harold: . . . and he's holding his annual Old People's Christmas Dinner at the Church Hall, and he said he'd be very pleased to see you there, providing—

Albert: Providing what?

Harold: Providing that you do not get Brahms and Liszt, and that you do not shock all those sweet old ladies there with your foul language and your dirty stories. The vicar still ain't forgotten when you did the crossword puzzle.

Albert: Dah, he don't know what time of day it is, he don't. Most of them sweet old ladies used to work down the pickle factory and the fish market when they were girls. I did four years in the trenches without hearing words like they use. It's like a stoker's reunion down them whist drives some nights.

Harold: Well, I think it's a very reasonable stipulation to make. Just behave yourself and you'll have a marvellous time. It'll be much better than with me. All those people your own age.

Albert: Same age? I'll be the youngest one there. Some of them old biddies are over ninety. There's three of them approaching the ton that I know of. They're old enough to be my mother, half of them.

Harold: Now, don't be stubborn. He's got your place all booked. *(Takes a ticket out of his pocket)* There's your ticket. That entitles you to a three-course dinner, an apple, an orange, an ounce of tobacco and you can see the conjuror afterwards.

Albert: I'm not going.

Harold: The Mayor's going to be there.

Albert: Oh, how exciting. He'll turn up in his Rolls-Royce. 'Hello, how are you?' – on to the next one before he gets an answer. 'Oooh that looks nice, I bet you'll enjoy that.' He won't have any, though. He'll be there just long enough to have his photo taken by the local press – him and his missus carving the turkey. He'll cut one slice and whoosh – out. You won't see his backside for dust.

Harold: Honestly, you talk about me being cynical, it's not like that at all. You should be grateful. You take the ticket and go.

Albert: You keep the ticket and hang it in the khazi with the wrapping paper. They can stuff their Christmas dinner, I'm not going. I've got my own home, my own grub and a son.

Harold: But I won't be here.

Albert: And I won't be there.

Harold: Why not?

Albert: Because I won't.

Harold: Give me a reason. Give me one good reason.

Albert: No.

Harold: Give me one.

Albert: No.

Harold: Yes you will.

Albert: No I won't.

Harold: Because you haven't got one.

Albert: Yes, I have.

Harold: All right then, tell me.

Albert: Because I don't want to embarrass you.

(*Pause*)

Harold: What's that supposed to mean?

Albert: Well, if you can't see, there's not much point in talking about it.

Harold: You can't just say that and finish the argument.

Albert: All right. It's for old people, ain't it? Who've got nowhere to go. No one to look after them. They all know about you. They'll ask questions. 'Hello, where's Harold, then? Off to Majorca enjoying himself? Left you on your own, has he? Oh, you poor old devil.' I'm not putting up with that. I happen to be proud of you, I'm not having people talk about you. No, it's best if I don't go. I'll stay here on my own so they won't know.

Harold: You can't stay here on your own.

Albert: I've got no option, have I? Don't you worry about me. I'll manage. There's plenty to do. I'll go down the graveyard and sit with your mother for a few hours, then I'll come back here, have me little bit of dinner, pull a cracker with myself, put a paper hat on and sit and watch the telly. I'll stay in bed the rest of the time.

Harold: *(sitting down)* You make it very easy, don't you?

Albert: It don't really matter. It'll probably be my last Christmas anyway.

Harold: You've been saying that every year since 1955. And you're still here.

Albert: Then you can go to Majorca every year.

Harold: You haven't gone and neither have I.

Albert: I don't particularly want to spend any more down here without your mother, anyway. I get tired very quickly these days. I've only kept going in order to look after you. And now you don't need me, there's not much point in hanging around any more. I might as well turn it in and go up and join . . . *(looks up to heaven)* . . . her. *(He gets up from the table)*

Harold: Are you going to join her now?

Albert: I'm going to bed. Might as well. Nothing to stop down here for. You'll want to get on with your packing, you won't want me round your feet. I just wish you'd told me earlier, that's all. I wouldn't have bothered with all these silly decorations.

Harold: They're not silly. They're very nice.

Albert: They'll have much better ones at the hotel. No, I'll just go to bed. You never know, with a bit of luck I might not have to bother about this Christmas either. *(He stops)* Oh, as you're not going to be here, you might as well have your present now. *(Takes present out of sideboard drawer and hands it to Harold)* Merry Christmas, son. *(Goes to kiss Harold)*

Harold: *(turns his cheek)* Thank you, Dad. *(Takes parcel to desk. He unwraps three handkerchiefs and a pair of Y-fronts)* That's just what I wanted. Really. I haven't bought yours yet.

Albert: Oh. It doesn't matter.

Harold: I was going to buy it in the morning. Something really nice. Something you've always wanted. I've been saving up all year for it.

Albert: Yeah, well, if I'm still here in the morning you can give it to me then.

Goodnight. *(He takes out a handkerchief, a tube of pills falls out. Albert looks to see if Harold has noticed)*

Harold: What are they?

Albert: What?

Harold: Those pills.

Albert: Oh nothing. Just something the doctor gave me.

Harold: What for?

Albert: Nothing, nothing. (*He winces and clasps his chest*) Goodnight son. (*He goes out*)

(*Harold sits at the table. He wrestles with his conscience*)

Harold: (*Shouts*) All right!

(*Albert comes back immediately*)

Albert: What!

Harold: I'm not going. I'm stopping here.

Albert: Oh no, son, don't stay here on my account.

Harold: No, it's all right. I never expected to go. Not really, I knew I wouldn't go. When I booked it up. When I chose the hotel. When I paid him the money. When he gave me the tickets. (*Intense*) I knew I'd be staying here. It's all a game, really.

Albert: No, son, you go. I'll be all right, really. I can manage. I wouldn't want to spoil your Christmas.

Harold: I'm not going. I'm stopping here. But I'll tell you one thing. (*He advances on the old man*) I'm not stopping here just with you. I'm going to cash in my tickets. And I'm going to blow it all on the biggest party that's ever been seen in this house. I'm going to invite everybody. All my friends. All the neighbours. Just so long as we won't be on our own.

Albert: (*beaming*) No, I know. I understand. Well, I'd better see how those puddings are getting along. (*He scurries out into the kitchen*)

(*Harold takes out the tickets and gazes at them*)

Harold: (*reads the front of the tickets*) Now with British Airways take an Earthshrinker to any part of the world. Well, if my world shrinks any more I'll disappear up the back of these. (*He holds up the pair of Y-fronts*)

SCENE 13

The lounge. It is Christmas Eve. Albert, on top of a step ladder, is fixing the old fairy to the top of a large new tree, beautifully decorated with lights, tinsel, bells, etc. The rest of the room is also fully decorated with manufactured chains, large paper bells and so on. The centrepiece of the room is a large trestle table with tablecloth and places set for a dozen people.

Albert gets a drink and sits on the steps. As he is about to drink, the front door slams. He hastily throws his drink away. Harold enters.

Harold: *(looks around the room)* Ah yes, that's better. That's more like it.

Albert: What have you got there?

Harold: The Christmas fare. Three turkeys, a York ham, and a goose. Here you are, get stuffing.

Albert: Three turkeys . . .? That's too much for a dozen people.

Harold: That's just the sit-down dinner. We've got the evening trade. There's another twenty coming in the evening. Then there's Boxing Day, forty-four coming down after the Skinners Arms has closed. This is going to be a three-day thrash, mate. Now, I've got two dozen loaves of bread coming, one gross of sausage rolls, fourteen jars of pickled onions, a twenty-eight-pound wheel of Cheddar . . .

Albert: And a new set of rods for the drains. Our pipes can't take that sort of traffic.

Harold: Don't worry, I've thought about that. That's why I've invited Basil from the caravan site. He's going to set up two chemi-khazis in the yard. With canvas windbreakers round them. *(He laughs)*

Albert: *(laughing)* They're going to need them all right.

Harold: Ah, do you know, Dad, this is going to be the first Christmas here I've ever looked forward to. I'm going to have a good time this year.

Albert: I'm not. I don't like having a house full of people. Let's spend it on our own, Harold.

Harold: You don't have to stay in here. I've told you. If you won't go down to the Old People's Dinner, I'm quite prepared to set you up a little table on your own in the stable. I'll send your dinner out there. You can sit out there pulling crackers with the horse. He'll look lovely in a funny hat.

Albert: Dah, it's a waste of money.

Harold: It's my money. My holiday money. It's not going to cost you a tosheroon. If I want to entertain my friends, that's up to me.

Albert: Exactly, your friends. There's none of my friends coming.

Harold: You haven't got any, have you?

Albert: All my friends were killed in the trenches.

Harold: Yeah, going over the top getting away from you. Gorblimey,

143

the war's been over fifty-five years, you should have made some more since then.

Albert: You'll find as you go through life you don't make many friends. Not real friends. You can count yourself lucky if you make two. Them what's coming round tomorrow, they're not friends, they're spongers, mate. They're just after a free dinner and a booze-up.

Harold: That's not true. *(He grabs hold of the old man and drags him over to one wall which is festooned with Christmas cards)* They are friends. Look. *(Points to the cards)* Fifty-five cards I've had this morning.

Albert: Exactly, this morning. Nothing till you invited them.

Harold: Fifty-five. And how many have you had? *(He drags him across the room to another wall. In the middle of the wall is pinned one little Christmas card)* One. One. And who was that from?

Albert: The Scrap Metal Association.

Harold: Exactly, the Scrap Met . . . haven't you had mine yet?

Albert: No.

Harold: I sent you one.

Albert: Huh.

Harold: I did. I wouldn't forget to send you a Christmas card.

Albert: Yeah. It'll come two days after Christmas, like it did last year. One of yours, with the writing rubbed out.

Harold: I tell you I sent one. It was a funny one. It had a horse on the front, and when you open it a cut-out of a big pile of manure springs out.

Albert: Oh, very seasonal. That's got a lot to do with Our Lord's birthday, hasn't it?

Harold: Oh well, if you're going to bring religion into Christmas, I take it you will be well in evidence at Midnight Mass tonight?

Albert: I might do.

Harold: Rubbish. You haven't seen the inside of that church since 1940, when you fell through the roof with half a hundredweight of lead stuffed up your shirt front.

Albert: That's not true. I was fire watching.

Harold: You were lucky you didn't get shot for looting. I'll never forget the disgrace of that. When I went to school the headmaster pointed me out: 'There is the boy whose father has had to turn his ARP helmet in.' The rotten sadistic swine.

Albert: I'm sorry, Harold, I didn't know about that.

Harold: Well, why do you think they chalked the swastikas on our front gate?

Albert: I thought that was because we were the only ones who never got bombed out. People get very funny during wartime.

Harold: Yeah. That daft little moustache you used to wear didn't help.

Albert: I had it before him.

Harold: *(doing Nazi salute)* Heil!

(Harold has wandered over to the wall with his cards on it. He takes one down, hands it to Albert)

Harold: Here you are, there's one to both of us. You can put that one with yours.

(Harold pins it up next to the old man's card) There you are, you've got two now.

Albert: One and a half.

Harold: Yeah, well, when mine comes you'll have two and a half. Don't moan, you've never had that many before. *(He picks up some small cards from his desk)* Now, let's sort out the seating arrangements. There's five birds coming to lunch. Who do you want to sit next to?

Albert: I don't care.

Harold: You're there. *(He puts a card down in front of a place)* Mr Albert Steptoe. How about Miss Sheila Figge on your left . . . *(puts a card on place to the left)* . . . and Miss Elsie Harmer on your right *(puts a card on place to the right)*

Albert: Ugh.

Harold: What's wrong with that?

Albert: I'd sooner sit next to the horse.

Harold: They are both very nice girls.

Albert: I'm not going to get much grub sitting next to Elsie Harmer, am I? Gorblimey, she's bigger than that ATS girl during the war. A twenty-eight-pound bird on the table and an eighteen-stone bird next to me. You won't have to do much carving with her around.

Harold: Yeah, that's true. Do you remember the way she ripped that side of beef to pieces on Guy Fawkes night?

Albert: With her bare hands. Frightened the life out of me.

Harold: I thought you liked her. She fancies you, you know.

Albert: Get out of it.

Harold: She does. She told me. She likes little blokes, that can't struggle so much.

Albert: You keep her away from me. You put her round there. *(Harold puts Elsie's card on the opposite side of the table)* Who else is coming?

Harold: Beryl, Joyce and Hermione.

Albert: I'll have Beryl and Joyce.

Harold: You won't, they're mine, mate.

Albert: You don't want two.

Harold: I told you, I'm going to enjoy this Christmas. I like to have one in reserve in case the other one flakes out. You can have Hermione and Sheila.

Albert: I don't know them.

Harold: Well, they're all right, but you'll have to be a bit careful. Keep your hands above the table, because Chris and Arthur fancy them.

Albert: Well, scrub Chris and Arthur out then.

Harold: I can't, they're bringing them.

Albert: Oh gawd, I can see I'm going to be lumbered with Gargantua.

Harold: Don't worry about it. If I see her carrying you upstairs, I'll blow the whistle. Now let's see, what else? Did you cut the fruit up for the punch?

Albert: Yeah, it's in the punch bowl.

Harold: Well, go and bring it in. We'll make it tonight, give the fruit a chance to ferment.

(Albert goes to get the punch bowl. Harold opens a few bottles of various spirits)

Harold: This lot'll make their eyes water. Oh yes, if I don't enjoy it this year it won't be for want of trying.

(Albert comes back, carrying a large porcelain po)

Albert: There you are.

Harold: What's that? I told you to buy a punch bowl.

Albert: Why waste money when you've got one of these? It's big enough.

Harold: I can't serve my fruit sangria out of a po.

Albert: Why not? It's never been used.

Harold: I don't care whether it's been used or not. Well, I do actually, but that's not the point. It's the principle of the thing. I mean, ladling the stuff out of there is going to look very choice. Hermione isn't going to reckon it for a start. She's a young Conservative.

Albert: What's that got to do with it?

Harold: Because at their do's they don't normally serve their punch out of a china po. They have silver or glass.

Albert: I don't think we've got a glass po.

Harold: A glass punch bowl.

Albert: No, we ain't got one. We could turf the goldfish out of his bowl and use that.

Harold: And where are we going to put him?

Albert: (*holds up the po*) Bung him in here.

Harold: You are not bunging my goldfish in there. He likes to see where he's going. Blimey, he hasn't got much of a life as it is, he likes to have a look out now and again.

Albert: He can look up, can't he?

Harold: He can't look up for three days. He'll have a stiff neck. Honestly, you know nothing about piscatorial anatomy, do you?

Albert: Well, it's up to you, you pays your money and takes your choice.

Harold: I suppose I could tell them it's an imported novelty from Harrods.

Albert: That's it. Come on then, pour the booze in.

Harold: All right then, I'll take a chance. (*He carefully pours in half a bottle of wine. Then adds a dash more*)

Albert: That's not much.

Harold: I haven't finished yet. A little gin. (*Pours a bottle of gin in. Goes back to sideboard*) A soupçon of grape brandy. (*Pours in a bottle of brandy*) A hint of vodka. (*Pours in half a bottle of vodka*) Just a threat of whisky. (*Pours in half a bottle of whisky*) And lemon squash. (*He pours in a little drop of lemon squash. Goes to the sideboard and gets a wooden ladle. Albert immediately pours in the rest of the whisky. Harold comes back and tastes the mixture. He shakes his head. Albert shakes his head*) Hmmmm. (*He goes to sideboard. Albert fills a glass. Harold takes a bottle of Angostura bitters and shakes in two drops. He tastes the punch. Albert waits expectantly*) Perfect. A couple of glasses of that and they'll be legless. Roll on tomorrow afternoon. (*Puts cloth over po. Albert crosses to desk*) That's right. Get the birds stuffed and put one of them in the oven. And before you say something vulgar, I am referring to the dinner. Do the goose first, it'll take longer.

Albert: Right. (*He takes the goose and goes to the door*)

Harold: And don't leave your rubber glove in it. Like you did last year.

(*Albert gestures with the goose*)

Harold: And you!

SCENE 14

The lounge. It is Christmas morning. The table is set up ready for the guests, with paper napkins in the glasses, a bowl of fruit in the middle, etc.

Harold enters, humming happily. He is wearing his best suit and carrying a parcel. He takes a pen and writes on the parcel.

Harold: *(as he writes)* To Dad . . . with love . . . no . . . *(he scrubs out the word 'love')* To Dad . . . wishing you a merry Christmas, and many of . . . no *(he scrubs out the 'and many of'. He turns the parcel over and writes on the other side)* To Dad . . . from Harold. *(He puts the parcel under the Christmas tree. He sniffs)* Oh, what a glorious smell. Ahh, Bisto! *(Shouts)* Come on, Dad, it's Christmas. We've got work to do. Stop stinking in that pit. *(Sings)* Oh what a beautiful morning . . . oh well . . . *(pours himself a drink from his optics)* might as well start as I mean to go on. *(He swallows the drink. Shouts)* Dad, they'll be here soon.

(Albert enters in his dressing-gown. His face is covered in spots)

Albert: Harold.

(Harold turns)

Harold: Good morning, Father, a very merry Christmas to you. I'm sorry about all the rotten, vicious, nasty things I've said over the past year and . . . *(he suddenly sees the spots)* What's your game? What's all that on your face?

Albert: I don't know, Harold. It's all up me arms as well. And all up me legs. And across me belly. And all round me—

Harold: What is it?

Albert: I don't know. I think I've got chicken pox.

(Harold goes over and stares at his face)

Harold: Chicken pox? You can't have. *(Albert nods slowly)* You can't have chicken pox. *(He runs over to his library and selects a book. He rummages through it)* It can't be chicken pox. Chicken pox. C . . . C . . . A . . . Catalepsy . . . coronary . . . cholera . . . chicken pox. *(He reads, muttering, then goes up and looks at the old man's face)* You've got chicken pox. *(Albert nods again)* How can you have chicken pox at your age?

Albert: I never had it before.

Harold: Why not, you silly great . . . you can't have chicken pox. We're having a party. How can it be chicken pox? Everybody's had chicken pox.

Albert: You haven't.

Harold: I must have done. When I was little . . . surely. (*He starts scratching his arm, without realizing it*) Nobody has chicken pox at our age, I mean, it's ridiculous. We've got people coming round. You'll have to go out in the stable and stay there. (*Harold starts scratching his chest*) If the horse catches it that's bad luck. I'll keep quiet about it, I won't mention it, I'll say you've gone away. You can't stay in here, you're contagious. Get out . . .

Albert: I'll wear my gloves. And me balaclava helmet. I'll put some flour over my face.

(*Harold is now scratching himself more vigorously. He realizes that he is scratching himself. His face drops. He opens his shirt front and looks at his chest. It is covered in spots.*

Harold: You rotten stinking old git, you've given it to me! Look, spots! You've done this on purpose. You've deliberately gone and given me chicken pox.

Albert: I didn't know, Harold . . .

Harold: I'll kill you. If you get better, I'll kill you.

(*The doorbell rings*)

Harold: They've arrived.

Albert: They can't come in.

(*Harold goes to the door. Albert pulls him back*)

Albert: We'll both go out into the stable.

Harold: I'm not spending Christmas in the stable.

Albert: Jesus did.

Harold: His dad didn't have chicken pox, did he? (*He throws Albert aside*)

SCENE 15
The hall. Harold goes to the front door and lifts up the letter box.

Harold: Hello.

SCENE 16
The yard/hall. The ten guests are in the yard, loaded up with presents, bottles, etc. They look round for the voice.

Girl: (*points*) There he is.
Man: (*bends down*) Come on, Harold, open up.
Harold: (*inside*) There's a slight problem.

Second man: Hello, he's started playing games already. Cor, this is going to be good.

Girl: Open up, Harold, I've got something for you.

Harold: *(inside)* There has been a slight technical hitch ... how many of you have had chicken pox?

Man: Chicken what?

Harold: *(inside)* We've got chicken pox.

Second girl: We thought you had turkey.

Harold: *(inside)* No, I'm serious. We've got chicken pox. Me and my Dad.

First man: *(to the others)* Who's had chicken pox?

(They all move back from the door. They consult: 'I don't know' – 'Have you had it?' – 'I think so' – 'I'm not sure' – 'I'll have to ask me mum')

Harold: *(inside)* If any of you have had it, I think it's all right for you to come in.

(They consult. None of them fancies it)

Girl: I'm not going in.

Second girl: You come out in spots.

Third girl: No thank you, not me.

Man: Well, what are we going to do, then?

Harold: *(inside)* If you've had it, I think it'll be all right. I don't think you can get it twice.

Fourth girl: I'm not going in there.

First man: I'll tell you what, Harold. Don't worry about it. We'll see you next year.

Harold: *(inside)* I can't quite hear. I'll come out.

(They all jump back a few feet)

First man: No, it's all right, Harold, don't bother, we'll be all right. *(To the others)* Come on, we'll go round my Mum's. She won't mind.

(They back away. Harold comes out)

First man: Cheerio, Harold, Merry Christmas.

The others: 'Cheerio' – 'Merry Christmas' – 'Happy New Year' – 'Goodbye' – etc.

(They all get out of the yard as fast as they can. Pause. Harold looks round the yard. He goes back in, then comes out with a can of paint and a brush. He paints a yellow cross on the door. He shuts it.)

SCENE 17

The lounge. Harold and Albert are sitting at the table, both wearing paper hats. Their faces are covered in spots. The table is laden with food. Albert offers Harold a cracker. Harold takes it. They struggle to pull it. Harold pulls the old man onto the table, takes him by the scruff of the neck and shoves his face into the sherry trifle.

And So To Bed

First transmission 11 September 1974

And So To Bed featured
Lynn Farleigh as Marcia
with Angus Mackay
and was produced by Douglas Argent

SCENE 1
Albert's bedroom. Close-up of a glass of water. A pair of false teeth are dropped in, followed by a Steradent tablet. The water starts bubbling. Albert is sitting up in bed, cobbling with a hammer on a large iron last with three feet on it. He stops cobbling and takes a swig out of the tooth glass, then resumes cobbling.

SCENE 2
The lounge. Harold is sitting on the sofa with Marcia, a woman of about thirty. The sound of Albert's cobbling comes from upstairs. Harold looks up to the ceiling, fed up. Marcia, also fed up, looks up to the ceiling, then at her watch. She sighs impatiently.

Harold: Would you care for another date? (*He offers her one on a plastic fork*)

Marcia: (*bored*) No thanks. (*Harold puts his arm round her and tries to kiss her. She pushes him off*) Look, we've done all that bit. When are we going upstairs?

Harold: I told you, we've got to give him a chance to get to sleep. If he knows I've got a woman in here, he'll be a nuisance all night long. He won't give us a minute's peace. He'll be up and down those stairs like a bleeding yo-yo. He'll find some excuse to come in.

    (*The cobbling continues*)

Marcia: What's he doing, anyway?

Harold: He's cobbling.

Marcia: What, in bed?

Harold: Oh, yes. Well, at his age there's not much else he can do. That's why he doesn't like me doing it.

Marcia: How long does he keep this up?

Harold: It depends on how many boots he's got to mend. I brought home six and a half pairs today. He's like a little gnome. He won't go to sleep till he's finished them.

Marcia: I can't hang about that long. Let's go up now.

Harold: I can't concentrate with him banging away all night.

Marcia: Well, it looks like he's the only one going to. Look, let's forget it, I'll go home.

Harold: No, no, don't go, Marcia, he won't be long. (*Puts his arm round her again*) This is all right, this is nice and comfortable.

Marcia: On a couch? You're joking. I've served my apprenticeship. I gave up the front room bit years ago. I like a bit of comfort these days.

(*The cobbling stops. They look up to the ceiling*)

Harold: Hang on.

(*They wait. Nothing happens. They start to get up, the cobbling starts again, they sit down again*)

Marcia: Oh, I'm not putting up with this. You can't hear yourself talk. (*She starts to get up*)

Harold: (*restraining her*) No, really, it won't go on much longer. Let me get you another drink?

Marcia: No, don't bother. We've done a bottle in already. I didn't come here to booze. I can't understand you.

Harold: What?

Marcia: You say you've been after me for months . . .

Harold: Oh, I have, Marcia, I have. Ever since I saw you outside the cinema. I looked up and there you were – up a ladder, putting up next week's film titles.

Marcia: Yeah, that's right, and I dropped a letter E on your head. (*They both laugh*)

Harold: Yeah, that's right. You were taking down *Naughty Knickers* and *Lash of Lust* and putting up *Herbie Rides Again*, 'cos the kids were on holiday. And you said I looked like Robert Redford. I've never forgotten it. I've thought about you ever since.

Marcia: It took you long enough to talk to me, didn't it?

Harold: Well, I didn't like to. I bought loads of choc ices off you but . . . I suppose it was that . . . on your finger.

Marcia: (*fingers her wedding ring*) Oh that. You don't want to take any notice of that.

Harold: I steer clear of married women as a rule. I don't like the idea of splitting up families.

Marcia: Huh!

Harold: Doesn't your husband mind . . . you know, you going with other men?

Marcia: No. We've got an understanding. We're a couple of swingers. We're a very liberated couple. Well, in fact, I'm more liberated than he is.

Harold: Are you?

Marcia: Yeah. He's in jail. Grievous bodily harm.

Harold: *(pulls back)* Oh.

Marcia: Don't worry, he couldn't care less.

(Harold goes back to her and tries to kiss her again)

Marcia: Look, I haven't come all this way just for a kiss and a cuddle and a box of dates. That's no good to a grown woman. We have other needs. Is there something wrong with you? You're not impudent, are you?

Harold: Impudent? Oh – impotent – no, of course not. I've never had any complaints. *(Sexy)* I don't suppose you have, either.

Marcia: *(leans into him provocatively)* Let's put it this way – you might have to take the day off tomorrow.

Harold: Let's make it a week. *(He chuckles in anticipation)*

Marcia: *(softly)* Come on, let's go up.

Harold: I'd rather not go up there while he's awake.

Marcia: Well, go up and hit him over the head with his hammer.

Harold: Oh, don't think I wouldn't like to. *(The cobbling stops. They pause. Nothing happens. They look up)* I think he's finished. *(They wait)* I'll go and see. *(He goes into the hall, calls up the stairs)* Dad, Dad – are you awake? *(He goes back into the lounge. Whispers)* Come on.

Marcia: About time.

SCENE 3
The hall and stairs. Harold turns off light in hall.

Marcia: I can't see a bleeding thing.

Harold: *(takes her by the hand)* Shush . . . *(He puts his finger over his lips. Marcia reacts impatiently. Harold leads her up the stairs on tiptoe, along the landing, and into his room. He closes the door quietly)*

SCENE 4
Harold's bedroom. Harold locks the door.

Harold: Well, here we are. (*Starts taking his jacket off*) This is it.

Marcia: (*looking round, not impressed*) Let's go downstairs.

Harold: No, no, you'll find it quite conducive ... once the light's out.

Marcia: (*goes to the bed and presses her hand on it, testing it*) It's got lumps in it.

Harold: That's all right, they'll soon flatten out.
   (*She pulls back the sheets. She screams*)

SCENE 5
Albert's bedroom. Albert wakes up suddenly, jumps out of bed and stubs his toe on the last.

SCENE 6
Harold's bedroom. Marcia screams again.

Harold: What's the matter?

Marcia: What's that?

Harold: Where, where?

Marcia: (*points to the bed*) There. It's a bug. I'm not getting in there.
   (*Loud banging on the door*)

Harold: Oh gawd, it's him.

Albert: (*banging on the other side of the door*) What's going on in there?

Harold: Nothing. Clear off. (*To Marcia*) It's not a bug.

Marcia: It is. I know a bug when I see one.

Harold: It can't be a bug. I had a sulphur candle in here all day yesterday.

Albert: (*shouting*) Have you got a woman in there?

Harold: No. Go back to bed. (*To Marcia*) It's not a bug. Really it isn't. It's a ladybird. (*He collects it and cups it in his hand*)

Marcia: I don't care what it is. I'm not getting in there.

Albert: (*shouting*) Have you found some more bugs in there?

Harold: (*to the door*) It's not a bug. It's a ladybird. (*To Marcia*) They're very good for roses. (*Opens the window*) Go on, little ladybird, fly away home.

Marcia: Well, this one is. I'm not stopping here.

Harold: No, don't go. Come back. (*He grabs hold of her. They struggle*)

Albert: (*looking through the keyhole*) Put her down, you dirty little devil.

Marcia: Let me go.

Harold: Please, Marcia, don't go. There's no bugs in this house, I promise you.'

Marcia: Now I know what your father was doing with his hammer – killing them. Let go of me.

Harold: No. Look, this is silly. You can't go.

(*They struggle. Then they fall on to the bed, the bed collapses under them.*

Outside on the landing Albert is killing himself laughing)

SCENE 7

The lounge next morning. Harold is asleep on the sofa. Albert comes in carrying a tray with a large gallon-sized brown teapot on it, two mugs, some bread, an enamel bowl full of dripping, and two plates of sausages, eggs and bacon.

Albert: Come on, wakey wakey, rise and shine. Mother Nature is bestowing her bountiful gifts. The sunbeams are dancing on the khazi roof . . .

Harold: (*from under the blankets*) Get stuffed.

Albert: Come on, time to get up.

Harold: Go away.

Albert: It's eight o'clock. Time you were out on the round.

(*Harold sits up. He winces and rubs his neck. His head is on one side*)

Harold: Oh gawd, my neck. I can't move my neck.

(*Albert is spreading the dripping on the bread. He takes some in his hand and rubs it into Harold's neck*)

Harold: Oh, that's better, that's much better. What's that?

Albert: Dripping.

Harold: Oh gawd!

Albert: Best thing you can have, that is. Keeps the cold out. (*Harold moves his head round and round*) Yeah, dripping on your neck, goose fat on your chest, you can't whack the old remedies.

Harold: It's a wonder you ever got a bird in those days.

(Albert wipes his fingers on the slice of bread and gives it to Harold)

Albert: Here's your breakfast. Did you have a good night's sleep?

Harold: Of course I didn't.

Albert: Well, I said you could get in with me.

Harold: No, thank you. After three weeks of erotic anticipation of what I was going to do with Marcia, I really couldn't have spent the night with you. Well, that's another romance up the spout. I won't see her again.

(Albert is stirring the teapot with a large wooden spoon. Throughout the scene he pours himself a mug of tea wherever possible)

Albert: I've never seen a bird move so quick. She was out of here faster than a bishop in a brothel raid.

Harold: It doesn't happen to other people. Other blokes get it for nothing. Me, eight gin and tonics, the Mandarin dinner for two at the Acton Lotus House, two bottles of Nuits St Georges, plus VAT, a taxi back here. She does in the best part of a bottle of Dimple while we're waiting for you, and what do I get for it? A stiff neck and my bed smashed up. Apart from which, two sweet and sour pork balls rolled down my chopsticks, down the front of my new tie, on to my clean shirt and finished up congealed in the fly zipper of my brand new flares. I did wedge last night, Dad. I really tried. I was entitled to a result last night. It's this house. It's the kiss of death. I don't know why I bring them back here, I really don't. I was worried about her meeting you. I never thought about the bed bugs. And then the final fiasco – the bed collapses.

Albert: It would have collapsed anyway. Better when it did than later on. Are you going to mend it?

Harold: No, I'm not. I'm throwing it out. That mattress is going straight on the fire. *(Shudders)* Ugh, bugs. *(He starts his sausages, etc)*

Albert: You don't want to do that till you get another one. You won't find one on the round as easy as that.

Harold: I'm not going to get any more beds off the round. That's where that one came from. It's disgusting, using other people's beds. You never know who's been in them. No, I'm going to buy a new bed. From a shop.

Albert: Cost you a lot of money.

Harold: I don't care. I've never had a new bed. All my life I've slept in other people's cast-offs. A man spends a third of his life in bed . . . or in your case, two-thirds. He's entitled to a decent one. I'm going to get a new bed, new linen, blankets, the lot. If ever I bring another bird home, it's going to be right. I'll get something sexy. I saw a round one in a shop the other week.

Albert: A round bed?

Harold: Yeah.

Albert: How do you know where your feet are supposed to go?

Harold: It doesn't matter. They can go anywhere. You can point in any direction you fancy.

Albert: What about the sheets?

Harold: You have round sheets.

Albert: Who makes round sheets?

Harold: The same people who make square ones. It's no harder to make round ones than it is square ones.

Albert: I bet it is.

Harold: It isn't.

Albert: I bet they cost more.

Harold: *(angry)* I don't care what they cost. I shall get round black ones.

Albert: Now that's a good idea. You won't have to wash them.

Harold: Oh, I thought that would appeal to you.

Albert: Yeah, I'll have some of them. Square black ones.

Harold: If you have black sheets we'll never find you. I might get a bed made specially. I don't have to have a round one.

Albert: No, you could have a triangular one. Or a half moon one. Or a figure eight.

Harold: Are you taking the mickey?

Albert: Well, a bed's a bed. I never had a bed of my own till I was married.

Harold: No, I know, Dad.

Albert: There used to be eight of us in one bed.

Harold: Yes, I know, Dad.

Albert: Eight of us. Four brothers, two sisters, and my mum and dad. They're all dead now.

Harold: Yeah, well, they didn't have gas masks in them days.

Albert: Yeah, eight of us. Four up one end, four down the other. Roll the sheets back and we'd look like a tin of sardines. Hard days, they were. Do you know what we used to have for breakfast?

Harold: Bread and margarine.

Albert: That's right. Bread and margarine. That's all. In those days bread and margarine meant you were poor and hungry, not fat and frightened of dropping dead of cholesterol. We didn't even know what cholesterol was in them days.

Harold: You don't now.

Albert: We couldn't afford it. The only thing that kept us going was the free spoonful of malt at school, in the morning. I don't think I would have reached fourteen if it hadn't been for that. Everybody round here was little in them days. If you got to five foot four that was your lot. If you saw anybody taller than that he was rich.

Harold: You're taller than that.

Albert: Not then, I wasn't. I didn't get this tall till I was forty. People nowadays don't know what it's all about. Kids of today, they spend more money on crisps than my mum had to keep us for a fortnight. It's about time they brought conscription back. Knock a bit of discipline into them.

Harold: I don't follow this at all. What's that got to do with buying crisps?

Albert: Everything. Life is too easy these days. Too soft. Anything they want, they get.

Harold: I wanted Marcia Wigley last night. I didn't get very far, did I?

Albert: Listen mate, if they fancy you, you don't need a posh bed. Anywhere'll do. I never brought girls home here for that sort of thing.

Harold: I'm not surprised, with eight of you in the bed.

Albert: I wasn't allowed to. We weren't supposed to do it in those days. Rigid self-control, that was the thing. Respect for what was right and wrong. Honour and consideration for the girl . . . unless you were lucky. But never in the house.

Harold: Where did you go, then?

Albert: Out in the yard.

Harold: Oh, how romantic. The junkyard by moonlight. A setting worthy of Antony and Cleopatra. They had the Nile, you had the Grand Union Canal. They had a barge. You had a junk cart with the horse taken out. They had their pyramids. You had your ten-foot pile of old ballcocks and gas stoves. The inscrutable face of the Sphinx watching over you, or next door's tom cat with its ear torn off. What's to choose?

Albert: We used to manage.

Harold: I'm sure you did. Pray tell me, where was the Royal Bedchamber located?

Albert: Over in the corner. I used to lean twelve old trolleybus tyres up against the wall and we crawled inside them.

Harold: Oh, the erotic splendour of it all! A veritable tunnel of love.

Albert: It was very comfortable. A bit dodgy, though. I remember one night, things got a bit hectic and the tyres started moving and we rolled right out of the yard and finished up half-way down Scrubs Lane. You ought to try it some time – you could do a lot worse.

Harold: No thank you. I prefer the more prosaic approach. This morning after breakfast I shall pop in to the Bayswater Bederama, and I shall purchase the most comfortable pit in the shop.

Albert: I'll meet you there.

Harold: Oh gawd, if I said I was going to buy a pair of socks you'd want to come, wouldn't you?

Albert: I just want to make sure you're not diddled. A bed should last you for twenty years.

Harold: And if you embarrass me you'll be confined to one for twenty years, all right? Watch it, little Gnomey Long Nose.

SCENE 8
The 'Bayswater Bederama', where a selection of expensive beds is on display. Harold and Albert enter in their working clothes. An assistant goes up to them.

Assistant: The betting shop is next door.

Harold: I am well aware of that and had I wished to place a bet that is where I would have gone. As it is, I have come about a bed.

Assistant: We do not buy beds, we sell them. Now, if you wouldn't mind, we are very busy.

Albert: Where, where? We're the only people in the shop.

Harold: It's all right, Father, the gentleman is obviously under a misapprehension. *(To assistant)* A word of advice. Judge ye not a man by the apparel he weareth, nor by the company he keepeth, mush. I think you will find I have the necessary conkers to facilitate the purchase of anything you have in this place.

Assistant: I'm very sorry, sir, but we are very expensive. I just didn't want to embarrass you by showing you anything beyond your means.

Harold: Allow me to be the best judge of that.

Assistant: Certainly, sir.

Harold: *(walks to a bed)* How much is this one?

Assistant: Three hundred and fifty guineas.

Harold: *(swallows)* I see. Hmmm.

161

Albert: Shall we nip in the betting shop?

Harold: Shut up.

Assistant: It is exclusive to ourselves, made in our own workshops, to a very high degree of workmanship. There are sixteen hundred independent high tension springs in the mattress, which allows for correct posture and weight distribution of the body.

Harold: Hmmm. Three hundred and fifty guineas.

Assistant: That does include the bedhead, of course.

Harold: Naturally.

Albert: Will you take his old one in part exchange?

Harold: Please, Father.

Albert: Why not, you haven't burnt it yet. *(To assistant)* It's a good one. Horsehair mattress, there's a few stains on it from where his Auntie Ethel's kids were staying with us, but they'll come out.

Harold: Dad. *(He pulls him to one side)* Go and get me some cigarettes, would you?

Assistant: Allow me. *(Offers Harold a cigarette from a large leather-covered cigarette box)*

Harold: Thank you.

Assistant: Turkish on the left, Virginia on the right.

Harold: Most civilized. *(He takes one)*

Albert: *(taking one)* I don't want that one, somebody's sat on it. *(He puts it back and takes a Virginian instead)*
    (The assistant lights their cigarettes)

Albert: *(coughing)* Gorblimey, did you make these in your own workshops as well?

Harold: *(sticks a brochure in Albert's hand)* Sit down there and read the catalogue. Three hundred and fifty guineas? *(Pushes Albert on to a chair. Albert pinches a handful of cigarettes from box)*

Assistant: Three hundred and fifty guineas.

Harold: Perhaps you could show me something else.

Assistant: Certainly, sir. Perhaps you could give me some idea of what you're looking for.
    (They move off)

Harold: How do you mean?

Assistant: What kind of room is it going into?

Harold: A bedroom.

Assistant: Yes, but the decor I mean . . . *(he is leading Harold by the arm)* . . . is the room aggressively . . . masculine?

Harold: *(looks down at his hand)* Yes, it is. *(He removes the hand)* So am I.

Assistant: Good. Then that narrows the field. We don't want any frippery.

Harold: No, we don't.

Assistant: Or chintzy, like this. (*Indicates a brass bed with chintzy covers*)

Harold: No, I don't want anything like that. I've been trying to get away from them all my life. I tell you what I do like. That round one. I had a quick shufti at it the other day.

Assistant: Ah yes. The Pompadour. Très, très chic, n'est-ce pas?

Harold: Oh, indubitablement. Combien?

Assistant: Quatre cent livres.

Harold: How much is that in real money?

Assistant: Four hundred pounds.

Harold: Je regrette le lit est trop cher pour mon goût.

Assistant: Ah, Monsieur parle bien français.

Harold: Oh si, si, you have to in my trade. One gets a lot of Frog antique dealers poking around the yard. Les meubles merchants, trying to have the stuff away, thinking I don't know what I've got.

Assistant: You're an antique dealer?

Harold: Well, yes, sort of . . . in a way . . . mixed, you know – bit of this, bit of that.

Assistant: Then your home must be exquisitely furnished.

Harold: Well, there's a lot of old stuff in there, yes.

Assistant: Then I'm surprised you don't have a four-poster.

Harold: No, I don't think so, the poles might get in the way.

Assistant: In the way of what?

Harold: No, I'd be frightened of them hitting their heads in the dark . . .

Albert: (*calls*) Harold! This is a good 'un.

(*They swing round. Albert is lying full length on a bed, bouncing up and down. They rush over to him*)

Harold: Get off there, it's not a bleeding trampoline. (*He hauls Albert off*)

(*The assistant feverishly brushes the bed where Albert's feet have been*)

Harold: I'm dreadfully sorry, has he made a mess? No, no, don't do that, let it dry and brush it off after.

Albert: (*spotting the round bed*) Here, there's that round bed you were talking about.

Harold: Yes, I know, we've been looking at it.

Albert: This is no good, it goes right down to the floor.

Assistant: Most modern beds do, sir.

Albert: Where do you put the Edgar Allan then?

Assistant: The Edgar Allan? Oh, I see. We naturally assume that most people have separate arrangements for that sort of thing.

Albert: Well, we haven't. Well, not *inside* the house, anyway.

Harold: Excuse me one moment. *(Pulls Albert to one side)* Look, you are embarrassing me. I am trying to buy myself a bed and all you do is nick his fags, put horse dung all over his clean sheets and talk about putting pos underneath his Pompadour. Now shut up and behave yourself. *(Turns back to the assistant)* Shall we proceed? What's that one over there?

Assistant: Ah yes, that one. That really is a lot of fun.

Harold: That's what I'm looking for.

(They make their way across to it)

Assistant: It's not really in our line, but one can't ignore trends. This is a water bed.

Harold: A water bed?

Assistant: Look at this. *(He pats the bed and ripples run across it)*

Albert: Here, it's moving.

Assistant: Yes. The whole thing is full of water. It's incredibly comfortable. Particularly good for people with bad backs.

(Harold tries patting it. The bed ripples)

Harold: *(laughs)* That's clever, isn't it, Dad?

Albert: That's no good. They'll all get seasick.

Assistant: Why don't you try it, sir?

(Harold takes his gumboots off and hands them to the assistant. He lies down on the bed)

Harold: That's marvellous. It's so comfortable.

Assistant: It's like a large balloon full of water. It moulds itself to the exact contour of the body.

Harold: Give it a push, Dad. *(He experiments with it, turning this way and that, bouncing. He is delighted with it)*

Assistant: *(picks up a plug on a lead)* It can also be plugged into the electric circuit in order to heat the water in winter.

Albert: That's good. You can cook your breakfast without getting out of bed. Here, and put a tap in it, you can make the tea as well.

Assistant: *(chuckles)* No, I'm afraid not.

Harold: What if it leaks?

Albert: Yeah, it'd bring the ceiling down.

Assistant: Most unlikely, sir. The skin is very strong. An elephant could walk over it without it bursting.

Harold: *(luxuriating on it)* Oh, it's marvellous. It's like being on a lilo in the water.

Albert: At least you won't have any trouble with bed bugs. It'll drown the little bleeders.

Harold: I am very impressed with it. There's just one thing. What's it like for ... um ... er ... I mean, can you ... er ... does it interfere with, er ...

Assistant: It's very relaxing, eases bodily tension, medically thera-peutic ...

Harold: Yes, but till you get used to it, is it difficult to ...

Albert: What's it like for crumpet?

Assistant: Crumpet?

Albert: Yeah, do you have to keep one foot on the floor?

Assistant: Oh, I see. You will find that any activity one would engage in on a normal bed can be engaged in on this one.

Albert: He don't want to get engaged, mate.

Assistant: You will find the gentle undulations of the water beneath the body when in congress does have a direct stimulating effect when allied with the rhythmic ...

Harold: I'll have it, I'll have it. Sheets and blankets as well.

Assistant: Two hundred pounds. Come this way, please.

Harold: It won't affect my water rates, will it?

(Harold takes from his pocket three bundles of banknotes, very dirty and tatty. He gives the assistant two of them. The assistant looks at the notes with distaste, puts them on the desk and starts to count them)

Harold: One hundred and fifty pounds – fifty pounds. My card.
(He hands him a visiting card. The assistant looks at it)

Assistant: Oil Drum Lane?

Harold: Shepherd's Bush.

Assistant: Thursday morning. Good afternoon, sir. Thank you very much. I'm sure you won't be disappointed.

Harold: I hope not. Good afternoon.

Albert: He's a pouf.

Harold: Oh, you noticed.

(They leave. The assistant finishes counting the notes and with a grimace flicks them into the desk drawer.

Harold frisks Albert and gets the cigarette box. He comes back into the shop and puts the cigarette box in the assistant's hand)

Assistant: Thank you.

Harold: Thursday morning. *(He smiles weakly and hurries out)*

(The assistant, watching him go, opens the cigarette box and puts his hand in. He feels around, looks down and sees it is empty. He drops it on the desk with a gesture of annoyance)

SCENE 9

Harold's bedroom. The water bed is in position. Harold and Albert are standing by it. Harold pats it and watches the ripples.

Harold: Well, that's it. All set. I've told Marcia about it. She's never been on one before. She's very excited about it. She's coming round tonight to try it out. I think we've put enough water in, don't you?

Albert: Enough? There's about a ton of water in there. It's the floor I'm worried about. When you start that congress lark it's liable to go right through it.

Harold: I have tested the floor, the joists are quite adequate. Oh no!

Albert: What?

(Harold picks up the heating lead. There is no plug, just the open wires)

Harold: They haven't put the plug on for the heater. That water's freezing cold. Oh . . . I've got to go out on the round.

Albert: Don't worry, I'll put one on for you. We've got plenty lying about.

Harold: Will you make the bed as well?

Albert: Yes, yes. Go on, it won't be worth while going out if you don't hurry up.

Harold: All right. *(He goes to the door, turns back)* Marcia's coming round at nine o'clock. I want you in bed, the door locked, and no cobbling, all right?

Albert: Yes, yes.

Harold: And no listening up against the wall with a wine glass.

Albert: Dah.

Harold: I'll see you – tomorrow morning. *(He goes)*

Albert: Dirty little devil.

(He opens his tool box and takes out a knife, sits on the bed and picks up the flex. He tries to cut off some of the plastic sleeve, but can't do it. He turns and rests the lead on the bed and starts sawing

away with the knife. He saws away determinedly, then a look of horror comes over his face as he looks down at the bed. The skin of the water bed has been cut by the knife.

Albert leaps up and grabs a sewing box. He takes out a large needle and thread and starts trying to sew up the slit in the bed.

SCENE 10
The hall, that evening. The front door opens. Harold and Marcia come in, giggling. Harold looks round.

Harold: Oh good, he's gone to bed. Do you fancy a drink before we . . . er . . . hit the water?

Marcia: No, thanks. I can't wait to see it. Does it really sort of . . .? (*Does ripple movements with her hands*)

Harold: Oh, it's very sensuous. I'm sorry about last time, Marcia.

Marcia: That's all right, Harold.

Harold: I'll make it up to you tonight, I promise you.
   (*They go into a clinch*)

Marcia: Oh, Harold.

Harold: Marcia.
   (*She struggles free, takes his hand and they go up the stairs together*)

SCENE 11
Albert's bedroom. There is a chest of drawers up against the door. Albert is listening. He hears them coming upstairs, slides the bolt across, dives into bed and pulls the sheets over his head.

SCENE 12
Harold's bedroom. Harold and Marcia come in, switch on the light and shut the door. The bed is made. Marcia presses the bed. It ripples. She laughs, low and sexy, and starts to take off her clothes, slowly. She takes off one shoe at a time. Harold starts to undress, too.

Marcia: No, keep your cap on.

Harold: (*chuckles*) Marcia . . .
   (*They go into a passionate kiss, standing beside the bed. In their*

passion they fall full length on to the bed . . . and through it, into the water)

Harold: I'll kill him – *(He extricates himself, rushes out of the room and to Albert's door)*

SCENE 13
Albert's room. Albert is cowering under his mattress . . .

Porn Yesterday

First transmission 18 September 1974

Porn Yesterday featured
Anthony Sharp and Dorothy Frere
as the Vicar and his Wife
and was produced by Douglas Argent

SCENE 1
It is a hot sunny day. Harold is driving the horse and cart down the street in his shirtsleeves and wearing dark glasses. He is hot and sweating.

SCENE 2
Outside the Steptoes' yard. An ice-cream van is parked, surrounded by a bunch of jostling kids, all clamouring to be served. In the middle of them is Albert, who pushes to the front and gets his ice-cream.

SCENE 3
The yard. Albert enters at a run. We hear stones and rubbish being thrown by the kids and hitting the junk in the yard.

Albert: *(shouting back at them)* You little toe-rags! I know who you are. I'll be round to see your mothers. Borstal, that's where you'll end up. Bleeding kids, they've got no respect. They ought to be on training ships. Taste the end of the rope, do 'em a world of good.
    (He walks over to a deck chair. Next to it is a tatty old round table shaded by a limp, ripped old parasol. On the table is a bucket of ice, a quart bottle of beer, and a half empty beer mug. He sticks the cornet in the top of the beer bottle, then takes off his hat and overcoat, revealing old khaki shorts underneath. He sits down in the deck chair, puts a knotted handkerchief on his head, and starts to eat the cornet. He picks up a

paperback, switches on his transistor (pop music), turns on an electric fan, and settles back)

SCENE 4
The street. Harold is still on the cart, even more hot and sticky. He pulls up, gets down off the cart, takes a bucket of water from the back. He takes a swig from it, then offers it to the horse.

SCENE 5
The yard. Harold comes out of the stable. He looks at Albert, now fast asleep, snoring. He circles the table, looking at the beer, the plate of lunch, etc.

Harold: *(mimics Albert)* I've just this minute sat down. I've been working hard all day. *(Own voice)* So have I, Dad. *(Mimics Albert)* Not as hard as me. I haven't been off my feet all day. I've been cleaning the house, cleaning the stable, clearing up the yard. *(Own voice)* Oh, I am sorry, Dad. You really must take things more easy. *(Mimics Albert)* I'm an old man. *(He pours the bucket of ice cubes over Albert's head. Albert jumps up, looks around wildly)*

Albert: Who did that? I'll murder those kids. *(Harold laughs, Albert sees him)* You – you stupid overgrown kid.

Harold: Serves you right, you lazy little turd.

Albert: Lazy? Me? I've just this minute sat down. I've been working hard all day.

Harold: So have I, Dad.

Albert: Not as hard as me. I haven't been off my feet all day. I've been cleaning the house, cleaning the stable, clearing up the yard.

Harold: Oh, I am sorry, Dad. You really must take things more easily . . . There's one missing . . .

Albert: I'm an old man.

Harold: That's the one.

Albert: Fancy doing a stupid thing like that. I could have had a heart attack, a sudden shock like that.

(Harold takes a towel down from the clothes line)

Harold: Go on, dry yourself. A little drop of ice ain't going to hurt you.

(Albert starts drying himself. Harold goes to the parasol)

Harold: Oh yes, this is all very South of France, this, isn't it? Very St Tropez. While I've been nearly fainting on the cart. Where's

Brigitte then? Did she hear me coming? Pop inside to put her bra on, did she?

Albert: I wasn't expecting you home this early.

Harold: Obviously. So this is how the jet set live, is it? *(Picks up the plate)* The outer remnants of a sirloin steak. A green salad. Tossed, I might add. *(Picks up the remains of the cornet)* Ice-cream. *(Picks up the ashtray)* A panatella. *(Picks up the beer bottle)* And a quart of brown ale. Very nice. Do you know what I had? A corned beef sandwich, and a drink out of the horse's bucket.

Albert: I've got yours inside.

Harold: Same as this, is it?

Albert: Well, no, not exactly.

Harold: What have I got? What has the worker come home to? What has the Galloping Gourmet created for me today?

Albert: Shepherd's pie and bread and butter pudding.

Harold: Both dishes made of course from the corned beef sandwiches I brought home yesterday.

Albert: You're always on at me to save money, and food's very expensive these days. Do you know how much steak is?

Harold: Er . . . let me think. One and six a pound. At least it was the last time you gave it to me.

Albert: That's a lie. You had a piece of rump steak last Thursday.

Harold: Yeah. I don't know whose rump it came off. A bleeding rhinoceros, I should think.

Albert: *(looking at the cart)* What did you come home so early for?

Harold: I came home early because I was knackered. It is hot today. It is eighty-two degrees in the shade, and I didn't have a parasol and buckets of iced drinks on the cart to keep me going. I also do not have an electric fan. The only breath of wind available to me came from the horse's tail as he tried to stop the gnats from congregating on his bottle and glass.

Albert: You haven't brought much home with you.

Harold: How perceptive – you're improving, Watson. *(Goes to the cart)* Oh, I fully appreciate that three and a half yards of lead piping *(throws piping on to junk heap)* . . . and one broken water heater . . . will not keep you in the manner to which you are accustomed, but this could be quite valuable *(he indicates a 'What the Butler Saw' machine that is the only thing left on the cart)*

Albert: Here, that's a 'What the Butler Saw' machine.

Harold: Ah, you recognize it. That takes you back to your lecherous youth, doesn't it?

Albert: Yeah, you had to be sixteen to look at these. Me and Charlie Harris used to lift each other up. Halfpenny each. Better than the pictures they were, you could stop the handle.

Harold: I'll stop your handle in a minute.

Albert: Have you seen it, what's it like? Is it the maid having a bath, or is it the mistress caught in the rain and taking her clothes off in the woods?

Harold: I don't know, I haven't seen it yet.

Albert: Here, it's French: *Fifi et la Photographie*. I remember that one. It's red hot, that one is. She's posing in the raw, and the photographer emerges from under his black cloth with nothing on – except his socks and suspenders.

Harold: His socks and suspenders?

Albert: Come on, hurry up, let's get it inside.

Harold: All right, all right, don't get worked up. I'll have to tip some more ice over you.

SCENE 6
The lounge. Harold plugs in lead of machine.

Albert: Let's have a look. (*Starts trying to wind the handle*)

Harold: You've got to put a penny in.

Albert: I've got a penny, I've got a penny.

Harold: Old pennies.

Albert: Oh gawd. Bloody decimalization. I said no good would come of it. Thirty seconds of red hot porn and they go and change the currency.

Harold: Don't get out of your pram. Patience. Patience. Grace Darling to the rescue. (*He goes to the sideboard and reaches up on the top of it. He takes down a pot and empties it out on to the table. It is full of coins. Harold sorts through them and finds some old pennies. He looks at one*) 1904. Edward the Seventh. You probably knew the model, mate, didn't you? Well, go on, have another look at her. (*He puts the penny in the machine. Albert goes to look in the viewer. Harold pushes him away*) Ah, ah, ah! It's my machine. You can have your penn'orth in a minute. (*He looks in the viewer and turns the handle. He chuckles*)

Albert: What, what, what's happening?

Harold: She's not bad. She must be knocking on seventy-eight now. (*Turns it a bit more*) Oh dear, oh dear, how did you ever get

turned on by this? *(Turns some more. Chuckles)* What a load of old rubbish. Here, it's stopped. It's gone out. *(Bangs the machine angrily)* That's not right. *(Bangs it again)* Get going, you—
    (Albert points to a sign on the machine)

Albert: In three episodes, three pence.

Harold: Twisters in them days, too. *(He puts another penny in the machine)* Ah, that's better. Ooh, she's showing her ankle. Stop it, my senses are inflamed. Blimey, that must be the biggest pair of stays I've ever seen. You could make a trampoline out of them. Go on, that's it, get them off, girl.

Albert: Show us, show us.

Harold: Get out of it. Dear oh dear, look at the size of those legs. She could play for the British Lions. Hello, here comes the photographer. From under his cloth. You're right, he has got his socks on. You dirty old man, I can see your bum. Wait a minute, that's not his bum. He's got tights on. What a take-on. Oh gawd, it's gone out again.

Albert: Always does when you get to the interesting bit.
    (Harold puts a third penny in. Turns the handle again)

Harold: Wait a minute. That's not right.

Albert: What?

Harold: It's a different story. It's a girl in a bathroom, it's not even the same bird. The 1920s, this one is.

Albert: When?

Harold: She's nice, though. There you are, she's stripped off. She's on the scales now. Hello, the door's opening. Here he comes. The milkman.

Albert: *(slightly worried)* The milkman?

Harold: How ridiculous can you get? A crate of milk and no trousers on.

Albert: Has he got his apron on?

Harold: Yeah. He's taken it off now. Cor – dear oh dear.

Albert: Is he pouring the milk into the bath?

Harold: He's pouring the milk into the bath.

Albert: All over her?

Harold: All over her.

Albert: And is he getting in the bath with her?

Harold: Yeah.

Albert: Turn it off, Harold, you don't want to watch any more. *(Tries to pull Harold away)*

Harold: Shut up, I'm enjoying it.

Albert: No, you don't want to watch that rubbish, it's not good for you. It's disgusting. Exploiting innocent people for gain, that's all they were doing. Mass unemployment. Young men out of work for years. Nothing to eat. Not knowing where their next penny was coming from, leaning up against the wall all day, a bloke steps out of a big car, says 'You're a well set-up young man, how would you like to earn a fiver? How would you like to be in films?'

Harold: What are you on about? Be quiet. *(Laughs)* Oh, here we go, coming up to the last furlong – hello, what's he doing with the loofah? You dirty—

Albert: Harold, come away.

Harold: Oh he's doing his pieces now . . . you ought to see this, Dad, he looks a bit like you, in fact he looks just like you. *(He stops turning and turns round to the old man)* You dirty old man – it *is* you!

Albert: Now, Harold, I can explain . . .

Harold: It *is* you. That's you in there!

Albert: You don't understand, it's like I said, we were all out of work and . . .

Harold: How could you lower yourself?

Albert: You were laughing just now.

Harold: I didn't realize it was my father, did I?

Albert: We didn't have any food in the house. We didn't have any milk.

Harold: You put enough of it in the bath, didn't you?

Albert: I didn't pay for it. I brought the left-overs home, though. I managed to keep a quart back.

Harold: How could you do such a thing? My own father – a male Linda Lovelace.

Albert: I didn't know it was going to be like that. I thought we were going to make a proper film. I thought I was going to be on the Gaumont. Another Rudolf Valentino, that's what he said. I should have realized when I got there – an old photographer's shed in the Goldhawk Road.

Harold: Oh, very MGM. That's where I bought it from. They're pulling it down. They were selling it off. I just can't believe it – my own father. Oh god, what must my mother have gone through? She didn't know about it, did she?

Albert: Of course she did, that was her sister in the bath.

Harold: It wasn't! Not Auntie Rose?

Albert: Yeah. She died of pneumonia two weeks later. You mustn't blame her, it wasn't her fault. It wasn't my fault either. You don't know what it was like in those days. They were hard times. Everything we had was in pawn.

Harold: And so were you.

Albert: It wasn't really porn. I mean nothing happened. It was just pretend.

Harold: It looks like it happened, that's just as bad. The first two penn'orth were innocent. They were just a cover-up for the disgusting penn'orth you were in.

Albert: Dah, it wasn't that bad.

Harold: It was that bad. Supposing people were to recognize you?

Albert: What, after all this time? That was fifty years ago.

Harold: I recognized you. You haven't changed all that much. You were just as horrible then as you are now. You don't seem to understand the position this could place me in.

Albert: Ah, now we're getting to it. It's you you're worried about.

Harold: I'm entitled to be. If this got out, I would be a laughing stock. This could undermine my whole social standing in the community.

Albert: Hah! What social standing?

Harold: You know very well how long I have been trying to get into the Acton Hill Golf Club. Five years! It's bad enough being a rag and bone man. They are very choosy. No Semites, no Commonwealths, and certainly no sons of silent porn stars. I mean, even today they don't allow actors in, even ones who keep their clothes on. Oh no, I shall be blackballed straight away. Once again, you have ruined my chances to better myself.

Albert: You make me laugh, you do. You don't mind going to see other people with their clothes off. All them French films. That's all right, you can't get enough of that. They're sons and daughters of somebody, mothers, fathers. That don't matter. As long as it's not one of your own. Anyway, it don't matter these days. All the film stars do it. Marlon Brando, Oliver Reed, they've all shown their bums.

Harold: They don't do it for a fiver, do they? And anyway, how can you liken yourself to Marlon Brando and Oliver Reed? Look at you. *(Albert glares at him)* Repulsive. Then and now. There is a world of difference between an artistic flash in a highly-charged dramatic film and your performance. I mean, there wasn't even a story. A milkman – with a crate of milk and no trousers on.

Albert: They only lasted a minute. You didn't have time for trousers and boots.

Harold: I know. A penny. It's all so tatty.

Albert: I don't know what you're worried about. Nobody ever saw it. They censored it. They said it was too racy. There was a police raid. They destroyed all the copies. They burst in just as we were finishing *A Night in a Turkish Harem*. I was frog-marched up the Goldhawk Road in a policeman's cape and a pair of curly-toed slippers.

Harold: *A Night in a . . .* – There aren't any more of these things?

Albert: No, I told you, they were all destroyed. I don't know how this one escaped.

Harold: It hasn't escaped, don't worry. I am going to destroy it myself.

Albert: You haven't seen the rest of it yet. Go on . . .

Harold: I have no desire to see the rest of it. I have seen quite enough, thank you.

Albert: Let's have a look before you do away with it. I'd like to see it just once before you burn it.

Harold: Yes, go on, look. I think you ought to. See how disgusting you were. *(He shoves Albert's head up against the machine. Albert turns the handle. It finishes. Albert turns away, sniffing to keep the tears back)* What's the matter? Ashamed of yourself?

Albert: *(quietly)* No. Just . . . funny . . . seeing what you used to look like. *(He sniffs)* All them years ago.

(Harold is taken aback a bit. He tries to hide his feelings of sympathy)

Harold: Yeah . . . well . . . we all have to get old, don't we. It'll come to me one day. *(He breaks the tension by quickly opening the machine and taking off the drum of pictures)* Let's get rid of this lot. *(He looks at the pictures)* Oh gawd – 'How are they going to recognize me?' – it's even got a cast list on it. *Milk a Lady* starring Albert Steptoe and Rose Bunclarke. Auntie!

Albert: Harold.

Harold: What?

Albert: Can I keep one of the pictures?

Harold: No.

Albert: Just for a memory. Look at it now and again.

Harold: No. It's too inflammable.

Albert: Nobody'll see it. I'll keep it in my suitcase.

Harold: No. I'm sorry, Father. It's best you forget all about this sorry episode in your life. And I will try and do the same. I shall destroy them all.

Albert: *(nods sadly)* Whatever you say, Harold.

Harold: *(pulls himself together)* Oh, for gawd's sake go and get dressed.

(Albert nods and goes out of the room. Harold flicks through the drum of pictures again)

Harold: Poor old devil. Look at his shoulders, covered in pimples.

SCENE 7
The hall. The vicar and his wife come to the front door, enter and go across the hall.

Vicar: *(taps on lounge door)* Anybody at home?

SCENE 8
The lounge. The vicar and his wife enter.

Harold: (*still flicking through the drum*) I suppose it wasn't his fault, really. He was a victim. Just another prisoner of the capitalist tyranny. He didn't stand a chance.

    (*The vicar clears his throat. Harold spins round*)

Harold: Oh my gawd. (*He quickly hides the drum behind his back*)

Vicar: (*startled*) Where? Where? Oh, yes . . . er . . . I do hope we're not intruding. The door was open. I did knock, but you appeared not to hear.

Harold: No, that's quite all right, come in. Oh, you are in.

Vicar: Something interesting?

Harold: No, no. (*He looks for somewhere to put the pictures, puts them back into the machine and slams it shut*) Just something I picked up off the round. Well, anyway, good afternoon, Vicar – Mrs Vicar – er – Mrs Cakebread. This is a pleasant surprise.

    (*Albert walks into the room. He doesn't see the vicar and his wife there. He is holding a towel in front of him. It is obvious that he has nothing on underneath*)

Albert: Harold, I've been thinking. If you painted a beard on all of them . . . (*He stands facing Harold with his back to the vicar and his wife. She looks away. Harold makes faces at Albert trying to draw his attention to the other two*) What's the matter with you? (*Catches on and turns round*) Oh my gawd. (*Gets behind Harold*)

Vicar: Ah! You can't catch me again.

Mrs Cakebread: It seems we have come at an inopportune time.

Harold: No, no, not at all. Father was just about to take his daily bath, weren't you, Father?

    (*Albert nods vigorously*)

Harold: (*smiling tightly*) Go and put some clothes on, Father.

    (*Albert sidesteps across the room holding the towel in front of him, making sure not to turn his back on the vicar and his wife. He reaches the door*)

Albert: I'm sorry about the . . . I'm sorry if you saw my . . . I won't be a minute. (*He backs out quickly*)

Harold: I do apologize. I wouldn't have subjected you to a sight like that for all the . . .

Mrs Cakebread: (*laughs*) Don't worry, young man. Charles and I spent our early missionary days in the Congo. Some of those chaps were built like . . . (*The vicar clears his throat*) Or was that the pygmies? I can never remember. Anyway, straight from a Dorset vicarage to there, a girl soon learns to take it in her stride.

Harold: I'm forgetting my manners. Please sit down.

Vicar: Stand and grow good.

Harold: May I offer you some refreshment? A glass of sherry, perhaps? It's very good. It's the one Orson Welles drinks.

Vicar: No thank you. We won't stop long. We've come about the church fête and jumble sale.

Mrs Cakebread: You know, white elephant stall and all that.

Harold: Oh yes.

Vicar: We wondered whether you had any old bits and pieces we could put on the stall.

Harold: You mean like my Dad. (*Laughs*)

Vicar: Every little helps.

Harold: Yes, of course. I'm sure we have something for you. I'm sure we could drum up a few old Picassos or Wrestler's Mothers.

Vicar: Splendid. I'll send the Scouts round to collect them.

Harold: I'll leave them in the yard.

(*The vicar and his wife prepare to leave. The vicar catches sight of the 'What the Butler Saw' machine*)

Vicar: I say, isn't that a 'What the Butler Saw' machine?

Harold: Yes, yes it is.

Vicar: I haven't seen one of those in a month of Sabbaths. May I – er – have a turn? (*Mimes turning the handle*)

Harold: No. No. It only takes old pennies.

Vicar: (*feels in his pocket*) I might have one – we still get them in the collection you know.

Harold: No, no, you can't. It's broken.

Vicar: Oh, what a shame. Perhaps we can get it mended. It's just what we're looking for to liven up the fête. It would be a good fund-raiser, that.

Harold: Surely not. Not at a church fête.

Vicar: Well, they're quite harmless, aren't they? Quite innocuous. We see much worse on the telly, don't we?

Harold: Nothing like this one.

Vicar: Really? May I – er . . . (*holds up his penny*)

Harold: No, no you can't, it's empty.

Vicar: Oh. I thought I saw you put the drum back.

Harold: No, no, they were blanks. A sort of test card.

Vicar: Oh, pity. Still, it's a nice machine, though. You wouldn't consider donating it to us for sale? They're very collectable.

Harold: I know. I was going to sell it myself.

Vicar: We could split it. Fifty-fifty? Sixty-forty? I do so desperately need new bells.

Mrs Cakebread: Desperately.

Harold: Well . . . er . . . yes, all right. Empty.

Vicar: Yes, of course. Thank you very much, that's most kind of you. Good day to you. The Lord be with you.

Harold: And you. Sixty-forty – you should need him, already.

SCENE 9

The hall. The vicar and his wife go through the hall as Albert comes back in his dressing-gown.

Vicar: Good day, Mr Steptoe. Quite an Indian summer we're having.

Albert: Well, there's enough of them living round here.

Vicar: Quite, quite.

    (Mrs Cakebread smiles at Albert. They leave)

SCENE 10
The lounge. Albert enters.

Albert: What did they want? On the ear'ole again?

Harold: *(he has taken out the drum of pictures)* Do you realize he nearly had a look at these? They're going on the fire now. They're too dangerous to be left lying around. *(Takes them to the door, turns)* I tell you, there's not going to be no phoenix rising from these bleedin' ashes.

    (Albert flaps his arms)

SCENE 11
The church hall. The fête is in progress. There are stalls all round the hall. The 'What the Butler Saw' machine is up against one wall. There is a long queue of people waiting to have a look.

    The vicar is looking on, beaming. Albert and Harold enter.

Albert: Let's join the tea queue.

Harold: Is this the tea queue?

Man: You must be joking.

Vicar: Mr Steptoe, how can I thank you enough?

Harold: What's going on over there?

Vicar: A great success. We haven't stopped taking money on it since we opened.

Harold: But it's empty.

Vicar: It was. You wouldn't believe how lucky we've been. Our foraging Boy Scouts while searching among the debris of a demolished photographer's shed in the Goldhawk Road . . .

Harold: Oh no.

Vicar: . . . came across, under the floorboards, an old 'What The Butler Saw' – er – thingamajig of pictures. What a success! We're selling old pennies at ten pence each and we've already taken over fifty pounds.

(Harold pushes through the queue followed by Albert. The people protest. Some women recognize Albert)

Woman: Look, it's him – the bloke in the machine! Let's get his autograph.

Harold: It's my machine. Mind out – gangway – maintenance. *(He reaches the head of the queue and pushes aside a youth who is looking at the machine. He looks through the viewer and turns the handle)* It's you again! In your curly-toed slippers. And suspenders. *A Night in a Turkish Harem. (Threatens Albert with his fist)* Right, that's it, show's over. All go home. No more today. *(They all grumble)* Go on, go and buy some white elephants.

Woman: Are you the man in the picture? Would you sign some autographs?

(Harold opens the machine and takes out the drum of pictures)

Vicar: *(coming up)* I say, I say, what are you doing?

Harold: The show's over, I'm sorry. Have you seen it?

Vicar: No, no, not yet.

Harold: You're not going to, either. Mammon, Vicar, Mammon. Sodom and Gomorrah. I'm surprised at you, letting your flock look at this stuff. I wouldn't show them to Parisians, let alone parishioners. *(Tries to force his way through the crowd)*

Man: Come on, put them back. My mum hasn't seen him.

Harold: Let go.

(They struggle. Finally the drum comes to pieces and the pictures are scattered. The crowd scrambles for them, Harold trying desperately to retrieve them. Albert is surrounded by women, signing autographs on backs of the photos. He is delighted)

Albert: One at a time. Don't push, I'll sign them all. Who to, dear?

(The vicar puzzled, but happy to get on the bandwagon)

Vicar: Autographs, shilling each, for charity. *(Harold comes up dishevelled, a few pictures in his hand)* This is splendid. I didn't know your father was famous. What's he done?

Harold: *(shoving a picture in the vicar's hand)* You might as well have one, everybody else has.

(Harold stalks off. The vicar looks at the picture. An expression of amazement comes over his face. He turns it over and reads the cast list. Understanding dawns on him)

Vicar: Autographs, *two* shillings each. Don't forget the bells. Come along, now. Get the star's signature.

(Albert grins as he signs away. Harold walks off. A woman approaches him)

Woman: Here, excuse me, is that your dad?

Harold: No, it's not.

Woman: Who is it, then?

Harold: I don't know, I've never seen him before in my life. He's a complete stranger.

(The woman joins the crowd surrounding Albert. Harold puts on his dark glasses, turns up his collar and slinks out)

Upstairs, Downstairs, Upstairs, Downstairs

First transmission 3 October 1974
Upstairs, Downstairs, Upstairs, Downstairs, featured
Robert James as The Doctor
and was produced by Douglas Argent

SCENE 1
Albert's bedroom. Albert is in bed. The doctor is examining his
back.

SCENE 2
The lounge. Harold is vacuuming, flicking furniture with a duster
at the same time. He stops the cleaner and takes out the full bag.
All the dust and dirt fall on the floor. He goes to the settee, finds a
dustpan under all the newspapers, etc, and clears up the carpet.
The kettle in the kitchen starts to whistle. Harold hurries out.

SCENE 3
The kitchen. Harold comes in and turns off the kettle. He fishes
out teapot from sink full of dirty dishes. He puts some tea in it,
pours in water, puts the lid on. He finds two mugs and lifts the
teapot. Whatever water is left in it pours out. Harold looks at the
bottom. There is a large chunk of it left on the draining board. He
looks at it in disgust, takes it out of the kitchen, across the hall and
into the yard.

SCENE 4
The yard. Harold crosses the yard to the dustbin. It is full. He
treads down the rubbish and adds the broken teapot. He collects
the milk from the doorstep on his way back into the house.

SCENE 5

The hall. Each of the bottles he has picked up has an inch and a half of milk missing, with the jagged remains of the silver caps still on them. He looks up into the sky, angrily.

Doctor: Mr Steptoe.
　(*Harold turns and sees the doctor standing at the foot of the stairs. Harold goes up to him, still carrying the milk bottles*)
Doctor: Having a bit of tit trouble?
Harold: Pardon? Oh yes. Little devils, aren't they? I leave a tile out there for the milkman but he never puts it over them.
Doctor: May I have a word with you?
Harold: Certainly, Doctor. Would you care for a cup of tea?
Doctor: Thank you, I'd love one.

SCENE 6

The kitchen. Harold ushers the doctor in.

Harold: If you don't mind the kitchen, I'm afraid the lounge is looking a bit like a motorway café at the moment.
Doctor: Yes, it's a lot of work to do on your own, what with looking after your father as well.
Harold: You can say that again. I'm knackered. (*He goes to the dresser*) I believe we do have another teapot somewhere. (*He takes out a novelty teapot – a clown face or a cottage, the more outlandish the better. He takes the lid off*) I think this is all right. (*He sniffs the inside*) Oh, my gawd, what has he done in here? You never know in this house. You'd be surprised what he puts in them sometimes. Do sit down. (*He pulls a kitchen chair out, and spots a half-eaten slice of bread and jam on the seat*) Ah, ah – excuse me. (*Removes the bread and jam*) You wouldn't want to have that stuck to your trousers, while you're doing your rounds. (*Chuckles*) The old bedside manner would suffer a bit – blackcurrant jam all over the counterpane. (*The doctor sits down*) And how is my aged Pa? Be able to get up tomorrow, will he?
Doctor: Er, no, I'm afraid not.
Harold: Oh. How long do you think?
Doctor: It's difficult to say. He might be in bed for some considerable time.
Harold: What, all day? I mean, he can do a bit of graft, surely.

Doctor: I'm afraid not. Not for a long while. Your father isn't getting any younger.

Harold: Neither am I. Are you sure he isn't swinging the lead?

Doctor: Quite sure. He's in great pain.

Harold: Only round his jaw. That's the only thing that needs a rest. *(Mimics Albert)* Do this, do that, gimme this, gimme that, get this, get that. *(Own voice)* You tie a bandage under his chin, that'll soon cure him.'

Doctor: I know it must be very trying for you, but I assure you this time he isn't at all well.

Harold: Oh. What's wrong with him?

Doctor: It's his back. He's got some disc trouble. He's in pain every time he moves.

Harold: He doesn't move all that much at the best of times.

Doctor: The only effective remedy is bed rest.

Harold: How long for?

Doctor: As I said, we don't know. It could take days, it could take weeks.

Harold: Weeks: I can't look after him for weeks. I've got work to do. I'm shagged out when I get home as it is. I'm always falling asleep on the board. If the horse didn't know the way home we'd never get here some nights. *(He pours out the tea, gives a mug to the doctor)*

Doctor: I'm sorry, Mr Steptoe, there's nothing we can do, except wait.

Harold: *(hands him biscuits)* Ginger snaps or custard creams?

Doctor: Try and look on the bright side. Sometimes these things clear up overnight. *(He snaps his fingers)* Just like that. *(He dips his biscuits in his tea throughout the dialogue)*

Harold: Not with him it won't. He'll hang it out. If he's that bad he ought to be in hospital. That's what I pay my stamps for. Bung him in hospital. I don't mind coming to see him.

Doctor: I'm afraid that's not possible. There is a terrible shortage of beds.

Harold: Bung him on the floor, then. If he's got a bad back, it'll be good for him, a nice hard floor.

Doctor: You don't seem to be very sympathetic towards him.

Harold: Sympathetic? Look, I know him. He's not as bad as he makes out. You say he's ill – believe me, if you put him in hospital, stretch him out on the floor, he'll make the quickest recovery known to medical science. It'll be a miracle cure. Like them Filipino doctors.

Doctor: It's out of the question. We only make use of hospital beds in an emergency. He can be looked after just as well at home. He may even recover more quickly.

Harold: Don't you believe it. Not while he's got me on the move. He'll try and get six months out of this. He'll be sitting up there like the Caliph of Baghdad, rubbing his bleeding lamp, expecting me to appear every five minutes.

Albert: *(off)* Harold, where's that tea?

Harold: There you are, he's started. *(Calls)* Coming, Oh Great One. Keep your turban on. There must be something you can do. Can't you give him a shot of something – like a .303? Have you tried acupuncture? I've got a tin of gramophone needles out there.

Doctor: No, bed rest is the only way. Bed rest and understanding. *(He gets up)* I'm afraid as he gets older this will happen to him more and more. You're just going to have to face it. He's going to need constant attention.

Harold: You don't have to spell it out. I can see it all, stretched out in front of me. I've seen it on the pictures. Plain, mousy, forty-year-old Jane Wyman devoting her life to nagging, moaning, miserable Dame May Whitty. Only in them films someone used to come along, Herbert Marshall usually, and he'd take her glasses off, she'd let her hair down, the old bird would kick the bucket, and they'd live happily ever after. Well, that's not going to happen to me. Nobody's going to let my hair down. It'll fall out before he's finished with me.

Doctor: I'll pop in again in a few days. In the meantime *(hands Harold a box of pills)* these are to ease the pain a little . . .

Harold: Thank you – how many do I take?

Doctor: They're for your father. And these are sleeping tablets.

Albert: *(shouts, off)* Harold, where's that tea?

Harold: You'd better give me some more, these won't last long.

Doctor: Well, I'll leave it to you.

Harold: *(bitter)* Thank you very much, you've been a great help.

Doctor: I've done all I can.

Harold: I don't know what I would have done without you. I suppose you'll be off to Canada soon? Sliding across the old 48th parallel, into the good old USA, getting in the back way, eh? Fifty grand a year.

Doctor: I beg your pardon?

Harold: Oh nothing. Just a few bitter remarks. I can see what I've got coming, that's all. Goodbye, Doctor.

Doctor: I'll call in on Friday.
Harold: Thank you . . .

SCENE 7
The hall.

Harold: If I can drag myself to the front door I'll let you in.
    (*The doctor leaves. Harold shuts the door and walks to the stairs. He stops at the foot and starts counting*)
Harold: One, two, three, four . . .
Albert: (*shouts, off*) Harold!
    (*Harold nods to himself*)
Albert: You don't care about me, do you? I'm ill.
    (*Harold starts wearily up the stairs*)
Harold: (*singing as he goes*) Oh God our help in ages past, our hope for years to come . . .

SCENE 8
The upstairs landing. Harold appears at the top of the stairs and comes along the landing.

Harold: (*singing*) Our shelter from the stormy blast, a crutch to lean upon. (*He arrives at the old man's door. Knocks*)
Albert: (*calls, off*) Hello.
Harold: Room service. (*He puts the mug of tea on a trolley standing on the landing. He takes a napkin and drapes it over his arm, opens the door and goes in*)

SCENE 9
Albert's bedroom. Harold enters with the tea.

Harold: Sir was the caviare, champagne and pressed duck, wasn't sir?
Albert: Where the bleeding hell have you been?
Harold: I'm terribly sorry, sir, there's trouble in the kitchen. The wine waiter informs me the Veuve Clicquot '55 has run out, and would sir mind making do with the PG Tips '74?

Albert: Never mind about all that, what did Crippen have to say? Don't take any notice of him. He's a liar, I am ill.

Harold: Yes, I know.

Albert: *(alarmed)* Eh? What did he say?

Harold: Oh nothing. Don't let's talk about it now.

Albert: What's wrong with me, what did he say?

Harold: Nothing, it's nothing to worry about. Forget it, put it out of your mind. You've had a good life, that's the main thing.

Albert: *(now very scared)* Harold, you're hiding something, what's wrong with me?

Harold: Don't think of the future, Dad, think of the past – those carefree golden days of your youth, those long hot summers, walking hand in hand through the meadows with a pretty girl on your arm, the butterflies, the rippling brook, the smell of new-mown hay, the smocked farmers drinking from their jugs of cider as they lean on their pitchforks taking a well-earned rest . . .

Albert: *(shouts)* What's wrong with me?

Harold: You're dying.

Albert: I'm not, I'm not dying. I've got a bad back.

Harold: I'm sorry, Father. I didn't want to be the first to tell you. I didn't mean to let it out. I . . . I . . . *(sniffs)* Drink your tea. Quickly.

Albert: What did he say?

Harold: He said . . . you've got three days to live. Starting from . . . . *(looks at his watch)* . . . now. Tick tock, tick tock, tick tock . . .

Albert: You callous little toe-rag. *(He picks up a pillow to throw at Harold and has a spasm of pain. He falls back on the bed, groaning)* Oh, my back! Oh, the agony! What did he really say, Harold?

Harold: He said you've got a bad back.

Albert: I know I've got a bad back.

Harold: Well, there you are, that shows you what a good doctor he is.

Albert: I told *him* I've got a bad back. I want to know why I've got a bad back.

Harold: Lack of use. He said you've got to get out of bed and do the housework.

Albert: No he didn't. He said I've got to stay in bed. All the time. Perhaps for weeks.

Harold: Oh dear. Well, I don't know who's going to look after you.

Albert: Well, you are, aren't you?

Harold: Me? No. I've just been on the phone booking up my holiday. I'm off to Cornwall for a month.

Albert: Cornwall?

Harold: Yeah. I'm going to do a bit of shark fishing, a bit of surfing . . . you wouldn't like to come with me?

Albert: How can I surf. I can't even surface.

Harold: Oh, shame. Well, is there anything you want before I pack?

Albert: You can't go. I can't move.

Harold: All right then. I'll tell you what I'll do. I'll bring up some tins of food and leave them on the end of your bed. You'll be able to reach them all right. Right, I'll see you, then. I'll send you a card. I'll leave the front door open and the doctor can bring it up when he comes round on Friday. Cheerio, I'll see you next month. *(He leaves)*

Albert: *(calls plaintively)* Harold, don't leave me. I'm ill. I really am ill this time. I can't move. I won't ask for much. Harold! *(He sobs in frustration)*

(The door opens and Harold comes in, wearing a PC's helmet)

Harold: Mr Albert Steptoe? I've got some bad news for you, sir. We have just heard from the Cornish Constabulary that your son Harold has been devoured by a man-eating pilchard . . . *(Takes helmet off and slings it away wearily)* I might just as well have been. I'm going to be eaten anyway, by a sprat. Here, drink your tea.

Albert: Thanks Harold. I'm not going to be a burden to you, honestly. I know you've got a lot to do . . . I know it's going to be hard for you. But I'm not skiving, honest I'm not.

Harold: No, I know, Dad. I was just mucking about, that's all. Just getting a few laughs before it all turns sour. Your pillows all right? *(He knocks them up for him)*

Albert: What else did he say?

Harold: Nothing more than he told you. You've got disc trouble in your back, you've got to stay in bed till it gets better, that's all.

Albert: How are you going to manage?

Harold: I don't know. We'll manage, we always do.

Albert: You're a good boy, Harold. I appreciate it, I really do.

Harold: Now, is there anything I can get you?

Albert: No, no, I don't want anything. I don't want to bother you.

Harold: No, that's all right. I don't mind. What do you want?

Albert: I don't want to be any trouble.

Harold: I don't mind, what do you want?

Albert: Well . . . I could do with another cup of tea, this has gone cold.

Harold: Yeah. Fine. *(He goes out of the room)*

(There is a pause)
Albert: *(calls)* Harold.
(Harold comes back in)
Harold: Yes, Dad?
Albert: Have the papers come?
Harold: Yes, Dad.
Albert: Could you bring them up with you?
Harold: Yes, Dad. *(He leaves)*
(Pause)
Albert: Oh – and Harold?
(Pause). (Harold comes back a little out of breath)
Harold: *(tenser)* Yes, Dad?
Albert: Do you think you could make a little sandwich?
Harold: Yes, Dad. What would you like?
Albert: Oh, anything. I don't mind. I don't want to be any trouble.
Harold: Well, let's see, corned beef?
Albert: No.
Harold: Cheese and tomato?
Albert: No.
Harold: Peanut butter and pickle?
Albert: Ugh.
Harold: Well, what do you want, then?
Albert: Anything, I don't mind. I could go a nice sausage sandwich.
Harold: We haven't got any sausages.
Albert: Could you go out and get some, then?
Harold: No. I – yes, all right, then. I'll go out and get some. *(Leaves)*
(Pause)
Albert: *(calls)* Oh – and Harold?
(Longer pause)
Harold: *(walks slowly back in. He is getting angry)* Yes, Dad?
Albert: *(embarrassed)* Harold.
Harold: Yes, Dad?
Albert: *(pause)* I want to go to the lavatory.
Harold: I can't do that for you. I'll go and get you a milk bottle.
Albert: No, that's no good.
Harold: Oh, gawd. We haven't got a bedpan. I'll have to go out and get one.
Albert: No, I can't use them. I never could use them. You'll have to carry me.
Harold: *(resigned)* Carry you.

Albert: There and back.

Harold: There and back. Three times a day. Come on, then.

> *(Albert puts his arms round Harold, Harold slowly lifts him out of bed and carries him out of the room)*

Albert: You're a good boy, Harold.

Harold: So you said.

Albert: Do you think you could bring the television set upstairs . . . after . . .

Harold: Yes, Dad.

SCENE 10
The hall and yard. Harold carries Albert downstairs.

Albert: And if you could pop down the library, I want some books changed.

Harold: Yes, Dad.

> *(They go out into the yard)*

Albert: And then later on you can go round to the off licence and bring back some beer.

Harold: Yes, Dad.

Albert: Be careful, you're hurting me.

Harold: Sorry, Dad. *(He carries Albert into the loo)*

Albert: This is very embarrassing for me, Harold.

Harold: *(closing the loo door)* It don't do me any favours, either. *(Sings)* Oh God our help in ages past . . .

SCENE 11
The lounge. Harold is in his working clothes, overcoat and cap, sprawled out on the settee, fast asleep. He is holding a bag of groceries in one hand and some hardback books clasped to his chest. It is obvious from his posture that he has just collapsed on the settee from sheer exhaustion. He has not arranged himself in a comfortable position.

SCENE 12
Albert's bedroom. Albert is propped up against the pillows watching some racing on the television which is on a table at the foot of his bed. Beside him is a sidetable with a big bowl of fruit and a pile

of books. He eats some grapes. On the bed is a big open box of chocolates. He eats one. He then peels a banana and starts eating that. He has an opened newspaper which he refers to with his pencil, marking his selections. Next to the bed is a bed table, the top of which can be swung round over the bed. On this is the remains of his dinner and a telephone. The phone rings.

Albert: *(picks up telephone; in a week voice)* Hello? *(Brightens up)* Oh, hallo, Clarence. Oh, terrible. In agony, I am. Every time I move. It's been a fortnight now. Harold? No, he's hopeless. I haven't seen him for half an hour. All he thinks about is himself and pleasure. Yeah, I'd love to see you. This evening, fine. Oh, whisky, gin, anything, I don't mind. I'm easy. Got any rum? Eight o'clock, fine, lovely. Eric and Arthur came round last night. They stayed a couple of hours. Got right Brahms and Liszt, we did. Eric brought a bird with him. About fifty. Her old man's just died. You can guess what from by the look of her. She's promised to come round one evening and punch me pillow up. Eh? No, not with my back, no chance. See you. *(He puts down phone, pushes table away, wincing with pain as he does so. He lies back on the pillows gingerly, then yells)* Harold!!!

SCENE 13
The lounge and hall. Harold doesn't stir.

Albert: *(bawls, off)* Harold!!!
Harold: *(sitting up in a daze)* Coming, coming. *(He gets up, still carrying the shopping bag and the books. Sets off the wrong way, turns and goes out into the hallway. He leaves the groceries at the bottom of the stairs and starts up)*

SCENE 14
Albert's bedroom. Harold comes in.

Harold: Sorry, Dad. I've just come in from shopping. What was it you wanted?
Albert: Racing at Kempton.
　　(Harold changes channels over on the TV set)
Albert: Right, that's all. I'll shout when I want you. Harold, did you bring my books from the library?

Harold: Yes, here they are. *(He hands him four books)*
(Albert goes through them, tossing them aside)

Albert: Read it, read it, don't like him, read it. Well, that was a waste of time, wasn't it? I've got nothing to read now.

Harold: I'll go down and get some more, they don't close yet.

Albert: And take that tray down, I hate the smell of food hanging about.

Harold: Did you like the steak?

Albert: Is that what it was? Terrible. All gristle and garlic. You know I don't like garlic.

Harold: I thought it would bring out the taste.

Albert: Well, it didn't. And it was fried. You know I like it grilled.

Harold: The grill's broken.

Albert: Well, mend it. You're not useless, are you? The peas were like bullets. If that's the best you can do, don't. I'd rather starve.

Harold: I'll do better tonight, Dad. I've got you a nice bit of fish.

Albert: I don't like fish. What is it?

Harold: Plaice.

Albert: Didn't they have any Dover sole?

Harold: Yeah, but they're about thirty bob a time.

Albert: Oh, well, if I'm not worth thirty bob when I'm ill . . . I'll make do with the plaice.

Harold: *(tight)* I'll go back and get you a Dover sole. Now, is there anything else you want before I go down?

Albert: No.
(Harold picks up the dirty plates and carries them out of the room. Shuts the door)

Albert: *(calls)* Harold!
(There is a pause. Harold comes back)

Harold: Yes?

Albert: What's the time?

Harold: Half past three.

Albert: Nearly tea time.

Harold: I won't forget.

Albert: Just in case.
(Harold leaves)

Albert: Harold!
(Harold comes back)

Harold: *(angry)* Now what?

Albert: Have you been out on the round today?

Harold: No, I haven't.

Albert: Why not?

Harold: Because if you recall I have been down to the library, round to the fish shop, up to the off licence, twice ... down the chemist's ... round to the grocer's and in between that I have been up and down these stairs twenty-three times. And now I am going out again.

Albert: Why?

Harold: To buy a hundred yards of rope.

Albert: What for?

Harold: I'm going to make a noose at one end and I'm going to put it round my neck and I'm going to put the other end in your hand. And I would be grateful if in future you don't shout – just pull. That way I shall know you want me, and also it might help me get up the stairs a bit quicker. Believe me, them stairs are beginning to look like the North Face of the Eiger.

Albert: Oh, it's wearing off, is it? I'm beginning to be a burden, am I?

Harold: No white man ever had a bigger one. But rest assured I will not fail in my filial duty. Now please, if you could refrain from wanting anything for fifteen minutes I would like to put my feet in water. All right? (*He leaves the room*)

(*Pause. Albert opens his mouth to shout. Just as he does so, Harold appears at the door and raises a warning finger*)

Harold: Ah, ah, ah! Shtum.

(*Harold shuts the door and leaves. Albert is fed up. He tries to listen to the racing commentary*)

Albert: He's turned the volume down. I can't hear a bleeding thing. (*He starts to try and move to the bottom of the bed to get to the television. It hurts him. With every move he winces in pain. Suddenly he gives a very loud yell. Then he realizes that something has happened. His back has clicked into place. He tries wriggling in bed – no pain. He gets out of bed and flexes himself. He does a few exploratory movements. Everything is all right. He does a bit of twist dancing. He grins with delight, jumps up and down.*)

Harold: (*calling, off*) Dad – how do you want your fish done?

(*Albert pulls himself up, a look of evil on his face*)

Albert: Grilled, with new potatoes. (*He gets back into bed and lies back on the pillow, grinning to himself*)

SCENE 15

The hall, kitchen and lounge. Harold comes into the house carrying some groceries. He goes into the kitchen and starts to unload them.

Harold: Oh, cor, I could do with a beer. (*Goes into lounge and out again. Goes to the fridge*) That's funny. There were two lagers in there this morning. (*He rummages around in the rubbish bin and picks out two empty lager cans*) I didn't have them, and I shouldn't think the horse has had them, so that leaves . . . that horizontal ponce upstairs. Which also accounts for last week's gradual disappearance of all the pink ones in my liquorice allsorts. (*A look of hatred comes over his face*)

Albert: (*calls, off*) Harold. Harold! Are you in?

(*Harold goes and stands behind the kitchen door*)

Albert: (*calls, off*) Harold! Are you there?

(*Harold shakes his head. He listens. He takes the shopping bag and creeps over to the larder, goes in and closes the door. The kitchen door opens and Albert comes in, looks round, goes out. Harold comes out of the larder.*

Albert enters the lounge and helps himself to a drink. Harold's head pokes round the door, watching him. Albert goes to the packet of liquorice allsorts and sorts out some pink ones. He pops them into his mouth, finishes his drink and goes out into the hall. Harold ducks out before Albert sees him. Albert goes up the stairs two at a time.

Harold emerges from the kitchen. He opens the front door and slams it, starts to sing. He goes to the foot of the stairs and starts counting to himself. He gets to '4')

Albert: (*calls*) Harold, is that you?

Harold: Yes, Dad. I won't be five minutes.

SCENE 16

Albert's bedroom. Albert is lying back in bed. Harold comes in carrying a tray covered with a cloth.

Harold: How are you feeling Dad?

Albert: Not so good, Harold. It's getting worse. I think I'm going to be up here for quite a while yet. (*Winces with pain as he moves*)

Harold: Oooohh, I am sorry. (*He brings the tray to the bedside and puts it on the bed table*) Never mind, this'll help to get you better.

Albert: What's that? Have you cooked me something nice for tea? Sausage, egg and bacon, is it?

Harold: Yes, you'd like that, wouldn't you?

Albert: Yeah.

Harold: And some bread pudding and custard?

Albert: Oooh, yeah! Smashing. And some Cheddar cheese?

Harold: Yes. Big bit, or a little bit?

Albert: Oh, all right. I'll have a big bit. With some pickled onions and four slices of bread and butter.

Harold: Yeah, and two tins of lager and half a pound of liquorice allsorts. Pink ones.

Albert: Eh?

Harold: You can have all that later. But first . . . *(He whips off the cover. Underneath is a bowl of hot water and a big bottle of surgical spirit)* You're going to have a blanket bath.

Albert: A bath?

Harold: That's right. Because you're a dirty little old man, aren't you? *(Dips the cloth in water)* You've been in bed for three weeks now, haven't you, and you haven't had a proper wash, have you? *(He slaps the cloth in the old man's face and rubs it furiously. Albert chokes and gurgles)* And most important of all, we mustn't let you get bed sores, must we?

Albert: No, Harold, I haven't got any bed sores.

Harold: *(pulling back the blankets)* A skinny little bum like yours is highly susceptible. Surgical spirit, that's the stuff. *(He pours surgical spirit on the cloth and throws the old man over on his side)*

Albert: Be careful of that stuff, it stings. *(Harold lifts Albert's nightshirt and rubs his backside with the cloth, hard. Albert yells and wriggles)* Aaaah – stop it, stop it. *(Harold pours more spirit on to his backside)* Aaaah – mind me goolies. *(He leaps out of bed and jumps up and down, yelling in agony)*

Harold: My God! The Saints be praised! A miracle cure. They'll turn us into a grotto. A grotty grotto.

SCENE 17
The hall, yard and kitchen. Albert runs from the stairs to the front door.

Albert: You rotten little bleeder – I'm on fire!
    (Harold runs out to the yard after him. Albert rushes to the hosepipe

and sticks it under his nightshirt with cries of relief)
Harold: *(laughs)* Up your pipe.
   (Albert holds himself, dancing up and down. Harold finally turns off water)